The Treatment of Mental Illness

The Treatment of Mental Illness

Science, Faith and the Therapeutic Personality

T. M. Caine and D. J. Smail

UNIVERSITY OF LONDON PRESS LTD

SBN 340 09493 1

University of London Press Ltd
St Paul's House, Warwick Lane, London EC4

Printed and bound in Great Britain by
Neill & Co. Ltd, Edinburgh

Contents

	Preface	6
1	The problem of general assumptions and value judgments in psychiatry and psychology	11
2	Basic assumptions of the psychiatric schools	24
3	The therapeutic community	45
4	A questionnaire measure of attitudes to treatment	58
5	The personalities of psychiatrists	87
6	The effectiveness of the treatment of chronic, hospitalized neurotics by the therapeutic community technique	102
7	Research in psychotherapy	133
8	Implications for psychology and psychotherapy	154
9	Conclusions	166
	References	175
	Index	186

Preface

Psychiatrists and psychologists are split, indeed fragmented, in their professional opinions on nearly every aspect of the problem of the causes and treatment of functional mental illness. Psychiatrists range from the strictly 'organic' and medical to the purely psychoanalytic and psychological. Both make their irreconcilable claims with equal confidence. In our own discipline of clinical psychology the basic orientations, technical expertise and treatment practices of two internationally famous post-graduate training schools in this country are diametrically opposed. Although the protagonists are equally concerned to appear scientific and objective in justifying their claims to superiority, 'science' has so far apparently been unable to resolve their dilemma. Underlying their differences, one is forced to conclude, are really very basic conflicts over values—a factor which many students consider when deciding which post-graduate course to apply for.

Some sort of value system is inevitable in any 'applied science', if only in the sense that it is considered 'right' or 'good' to apply science rather than faith, belief, dogma or intuition. In our day the superiority of science is, often with too little reflection, taken for granted. What does and what does not constitute 'science' is a complex philosophical question, an exhaustive discussion of which, though rewarding and even necessary, is clearly beyond the scope of this book. The scientific content of most applied sciences consists of hypothesis and experiment leading to a structure of 'established fact', which enables us to understand and predict the phenomena over which we wish to gain control. In psychiatry no such structure exists (it is even questionable whether it *could* exist), despite there being no lack of hypotheses which have given rise to conflicting and inadequate experimental evidence. We are thus left with values and assumptions, which, though they form the basis of treatment for the mentally ill, are obscured by spurious claims to objectivity.

This state of affairs is clearly not satisfactory, and yet the demands of reality force us to come to terms with it and to deal with it as best we can. If we have not yet evolved a suitable scientific understanding of abnormal psychology and mental illness, the least we can do is to attempt to bring some scientific light to bear on the treatment programmes which we have evolved—if the mentally ill are treated on the basis of assumption, faith and guesswork, we can at least attempt to elucidate the nature of these. If a patient knows that his neurosis cannot be cured *scientifically* (which does not imply that it cannot be cured at all), at least he can make a choice concerning the type of non-scientific treatment he might prefer.

Sundberg and Tyler (1963)* point out that there are cultural differences even in the use of the words 'science'—in fact, there are gross differences even within cultures—and go on to suggest that the first task of the clinician, both in practice and in training, is to discover the conceptual framework under which he is already operating. Whether or not the clinician subscribes to a recognized theory, it is his duty to make his beliefs explicit: 'If assuming one thing rather than another leads the clinician to ask this question rather than that, to look for certain things in a case history, to adopt certain attitudes and to ignore other possible ones, to make certain interpretations, or in general, to behave in one way rather than another in the clinical setting, these assumptions are important enough to include in the clinician's framework.'

It is the central argument of this book that not only is it necessary to recognize and define our presuppositions, assumptions and beliefs, but also that their generation is subject to investigation. The findings of such research will have very practical applications both for the effectiveness of training and treatment programmes and for the selection and adjustment of the staff involved.

The present book is built around our own attempts to identify

* All references are given on p. 175 ff.

and measure the attitudes and beliefs of both staff and patients in mental hospitals, in the setting of various kinds of theoretical orientation, with a particular focus on 'therapeutic community' methods of treatment. The first three chapters constitute an attempt to provide a theoretical argument for the cogency of this undertaking, and the following two chapters describe the concrete results of our endeavour. Chapter 4 is based largely on work already reported in psychological journals (Caine and Smail 1967*a*, 1968*a* and 1968*b*), while chapter 5 contains hitherto unpublished research findings. The problem of the effectiveness of 'therapeutic community' treatment is discussed in chapter 6, in which relevant research evidence, again as yet mostly unpublished, is also presented. The remainder of the book is concerned with a consideration of the possible significance of our own and others' research in this field for, in particular, the psychotherapeutic relationship, and what kind of future approaches might as the result be considered as fruitful.

It is hoped that the book will be comprehensible to others besides those concerned professionally with the care of the mentally ill. To this end we have made some attempt to avoid over-weighting the material with psychological jargon. Inevitably, however, we have had also to bear in mind our professional colleagues who will be interested in technical details, in particular as these are related to the presentation of our research findings. But even so, the more general reader need not, we feel, be too distracted by the technicalities of the research oriented chapters, and should be able to follow the general drift of our argument without too great difficulty.

We are much concerned in this book with the biases and personalities of those we have been studying. Levy and Orr (1959) recommend that the biases and personalities of the researchers themselves should be subjected to similar scrutiny. Beyond a rather bald statement of our position we have for obvious reasons been unable to do this. It has not been our intention so much to review the literature as to put forward an argument, and to this extent our discussion may be open to the charge of one-sidedness. But however dispassionate science claims to be, real objectivity is probably an impossible attainment. Our biases, we hope, will be abundantly clear from this book, and we should not wish to repudiate them. We shall be happy to relinquish them for 'better' ones if and when we are faced with evidence sufficiently convincing to make them untenable.

There are a number of people who helped us with various aspects of the research to whom we should like to express our gratitude. Dr Keith Hope gave us a great deal of help in the statistical analysis of our questionnaire data. We are also greatly indebted to all the medical and nursing staff who kindly agreed to complete our questionnaire and personality measures, as well as to the many patients who also volunteered to do so. Mr E. J. J. Price was particularly helpful in obtaining respondents for us, and Mr R. Kirkwood and Miss Ann White played a considerable part in gathering the data reported in chapter 6.

CHAPTER I

The problem of general assumptions and value judgments in psychiatry and psychology

This book has to do with approaches to the treatment and care of mentally ill patients. Although specific theories on the nature of mental illness and its treatment will be discussed, we are interested, too, in the more general assumptions underlying certain psychiatric and psychological orientations. Again, although we shall be dealing with some specific assumptions of psychiatrists, nurses and patients regarding the therapeutic ethos, there is a place for the discussion of cultural and institutional assumptions involving questions of the causation of mental illness, the responsibility for treatment, and the like.

There is a current tendency, for example, supported by successive Ministers of Health, to portray mental illness as fundamentally indistinguishable from physical illness, and to treat, where possible, the mentally ill and the physically ill in the same institutions. Undoubtedly this practice springs from a desire to mitigate the stigma of mental illness, which involves the isolation of mentally ill persons in large, inaccessible, rigidly controlled mental hospitals.

But to what extent is this policy justified? Are the inherent assumptions of physically oriented physicians and nurses really applicable to the mental field? To what extent does 'functional' mental illness really resemble physical illness, and call for the same methods of treatment and care? It is the argument of this book that, far from being based on 'scientific facts', the current approaches to these problems depend primarily upon the personal assumptions and value judgments of the people concerned, including the patients. These personal assumptions must inevitably be derived from psychological and sociological considerations.

Psychiatry is a branch of medicine, and as such it must share some of the features of the practice of medicine in general. Although medicine is frequently described as a science or as an art or as some combination of science and art, it is perhaps more accurately defined as a profession. As such, sociologically, medicine shares certain characteristics with other professions, characteristics which inevitably impinge on the beliefs and attitudes of their members. One of the central features of human institutions, which include the professions, is their function of control over their members. In fact, Hughes (1946) considers that the processes of institutional control are primarily exemplified by the professions. The members of an established profession possess both a technique and a body of knowledge pertaining to it which they apply in performing some service for other members of society. The relevant techniques and knowledge are systematized and passed on by formal means and in 'esoteric' language, with an accompanying claim that the professionals have the sole right to judge this knowledge and to apply it in their field of activity. A considerable problem of professional control, however, is that of determining who are members and who are colleagues. This problem is usually decided by delineating the task or area of activity, by determining the appropriate professional technique to deal with it, and by deciding what services are to be given. In psychiatry the problem of delineation, and hence of control over members, is notoriously difficult, and is the source of continuing friction both within the profession and between allied professional groups. There is not the necessary agreement, for example, on the nature and aetiology of mental illness either within the medical profession, among scientists, or indeed in our society as a whole. To this extent the medical profession has failed in some degree in its take-over bid for the field of psychological and social adjustment.

In the absence of any 'proof' to the contrary, the strongest argument for medical control is to assume that at bottom all mental illnesses have an organic basis and can be treated most effectively by physical means. This seems to underlie the view of Mowbray and Rodger (1963), who write: 'As medical knowledge increased during the past 100 years, the doctor's role as a personal adviser tended to be replaced by his role as a technician or administrator. At present when the doctor has achieved almost complete success in the treatment of infectious diseases (formerly his greatest problem), new demands upon his skill are arising. Consequently the practice of medicine is changing. One of the current changes is the increased proportion of the doctor's work now being directed to the care and treatment of patients suffering from illnesses which are either characterized by or engendered by emotional difficulties or which are prolonged by psychological factors. These illnesses are termed *psychoneurotic* or *psychosomatic*, and the rise in their incidence is often glibly ascribed to the changing ways of life, and to changed values in the modern world. Whatever their cause, the present need for professional help for emotional problems brings patients more and more to their doctors. The psychiatrist is the appropriate specialist, but many problems, which in their extreme or chronic form would be referred to psychiatrists, are resolved at earlier stages by general practitioners, who take an enlightened, sympathetic, yet detached point of view.'

Similarly, in the *Textbook of Medicine* (1961) Curran and Partridge write that in psychiatry mind and body are considered to be inseparable. Mental activity is regarded as a function of the nervous system and is conditioned by physical factors. There must, for example, be an adequate supply of blood to the brain, and the blood must be within certain limits of acidity and alkalinity and must contain certain quantities of oxygen and sugar. Thus mental activity depends upon certain physical conditions. Mind and body must not be considered as separate entities, but as together forming a whole. Mental illness, however, is shown 'objectively' as a substantial impairment of efficiency, or of the capacity for satisfactory social relations. Schizophrenia is talked of as a disease due to some hereditarily transmitted predisposition, 'although no morbid anatomy or pathology has yet been found'. In this view environmental stresses are only precipitating and are not causal. Innumerable other instances of this attitude can be quoted. The common assumption underlying all such attitudes is that mental illness is a disease which, in time, will be found to have some physical cause.

The mentally ill should therefore have the same sort of treatment and care as the physically ill.

Such views have never found general agreement. Professional medicine does not escape the presuppositions, mores and popular beliefs of an age or culture. Ambrose Paré, for example, the founder of modern surgery, was convinced that the devil caused women to behave like witches, and that witches should be destroyed not treated. The 'bad' not 'mad' argument is still with us, and the ancient link between the medical man and the priest is preserved even now: this is well illustrated by a recent broadcast on faith healing in which the head of the Psychological Medicine Department of a well-known London hospital remarked that after the necessary physical treatments, psychiatric patients were often referred back to their professional religious advisers for psychotherapy. Although, mercifully, the treatments meted out today by both medical men and clerics are different from historical procedures, are they any more 'scientifically' based? Do they need to be? To what extent are they still determined by, and depend for their success upon, the cultural ethos in which the treatments are practised, including the narrower tradition of the hospital concerned, the faith of the doctor in his prescription, and the religious conviction of the spiritual adviser, or perhaps some complex of both?

In their history of medical psychology, Zilboorg and Henry (1941) have made a plea for the frank cognizance of this aspect of medical treatment; they quote Emile Ittré, who wrote one hundred years ago, 'If the science of medicine is not to be lowered to the rank of a mere mechanical profession, it must occupy itself with its history.' Zilboorg and Henry make the point that the functions of the doctor are, in fact, dictated by the demands of his patients. Primitive man, they suggest, in his search for help to relieve sickness or injury—whether from the primitive priest, the shaman, the medicine man, or from magic or the fusion of herbs—was making the history of medicine. His demand for help caused the appearance of primitive doctors. 'It may be said with considerable certainty that it was not the doctor who by some miracle of spontaneous generation appeared first on the scene and, inspired by a lofty love for suffering humanity, sought to alleviate pain and began to make medical discoveries. Guided from the very beginning by the demands of the patients, the doctor had to respond and to serve; it was his business at all times and at all costs to supply what the patient wanted. This particular type of relationship between patient and doctor was and still is the most potent stimulus to the progress of medicine and surgery. . . . More often than not, the patient trusted and idealized his doctor. Even in later centuries, when the doctor abandoned his mystical communion with the supernatural spirits and became a layman, he was still considered an individual apart. He had to be a good man, an honest, pious, self-sacrificing person, one with more than a tinge of pompous dignity and social sainthood. . . . The Hippocratic oath is not merely a dignified formulation of the high ethical standards of one great physician, not so much his own original conception, but rather the expression of a tradition which ailing human beings had imposed upon their healers.'

Rather more than in physical illness, the popular conceptions of former times regarding the nature and causes of mental illness placed the onus of treatment in the hands of others than those of the 'earthy, materialistic, herb-brewing, and urine-smelling medicine man'. The presuppositions of society dictated other media. 'Before humanity began to presume that the initiated, the priests or the saints, could cast out the devil, it was considered a matter of course that the sick were in some way too sacred and good or too powerful for anyone to venture to reduce them to the unblessed state of normalcy. In other words, from the very outset it was taken for granted that medicine had no power, even had no right, over the mentally sick'—an assumption, presumably, which most medical men of the time would have accepted. Zilboorg and Henry presume that 'science' will confirm the present take-over bid of the medical profession—a nice instance, perhaps, of their own argument that the doctor's business is to supply what the patient wants. The twentieth-century patient wants his treatment to be 'scientific'.

Historically and theoretically it is probably true that the major challenge to the organic, 'strictly medical' approach to mental illness comes from the professions of the law and the church and from the social sciences. Barbara Wootton (1960) points out that in the eighteenth century no clear distinction was drawn between the mentally ill and the criminal. In France, for example, the Bicêtre and the Salpêtrière were known as both hospitals and prisons. The distinction between the two classes is still confused; but instead of treating lunatics as criminals, she remarks, we now regard many criminals as lunatics. A further confusion arose in the nineteenth century, when the care of prisoners' mental health was considered to come within the prison chaplain's province of moral instruction rather than within that of the prison doctor.

Both Wootton (and Halmos 1965) consider that the traffic in humanizing ideas is now reversed, and is moving from the psychiatric field out into society as a whole. Thus a 'psychiatric aroma' pervades the discussion of problems of antisocial behaviour, and 'at every turn the current vocabulary of social pathology (including that very phrase) bears witness to the degree to which concepts of mental health and mental illness or defectiveness now permeate our thinking'. While welcoming this as a humanizing influence, Wootton warns us that mental health and ill health cannot be defined in scientific terms which are free of subjective moral judgments. She considers that underlying the prevailing views regarding the relation between mental disorder and anti-social behaviour lies a series of closely related assumptions. First, it is assumed that mental health, or its opposite, are objective in the sense that they are more than an expression either of the tastes and value judgments of psychiatrists or of the cultural norms of a society: mental illness is closely analogous to physical illness, and is no less 'real' and objective. Further, this hypothetically diagnosable mental illness may account for some socially unacceptable behaviour, and may thus diminish moral responsibility. But not all deviant behaviour is explicable or excusable in this way. Such views, she maintains, represent a desire to assimilate attitudes to mental and to physical health as far as possible, and to guarantee that mental illness shall give the same protection from blame as physical illness already gives.

In examining some twenty odd definitions of mental health, certain recurrent themes emerged, namely, that mental health tended to be equated with happiness, preferably of a 'higher' order, with vigour, with the full use of capabilities, with integration in the sense of freedom from conflict within oneself, and with harmonious adjustment to the environment. The difficulty here is, as Wootton points out, the conflict between 'health' and 'morals'. The sadist or the masochist might qualify as mentally healthy under brutal environmental régimes. If, on the other hand, the definitions apply only in specific social conditions, then the claim of mental health to rank as an objective, natural condition, independent of personal tastes, value judgments and cultural norms, must be rejected. 'Indeed, so long as mental health is defined in terms that are independent of moral or social virtue, it is to be anticipated that there will be some persons who enjoy tolerably good mental health, but whose social behaviour leaves much to be desired, just as there are many others in excellent physical health of whom the same can be said. Mental health is, no doubt, in itself a desirable aim, and its promotion a proper goal of social policy. But, so long as it is defined in terms that are independent of socially approved behaviour, it can rank as only one amongst many possible social goals, between which there may at times be conflict. The analogy with physical health, of which exactly the same is true, is conspicuously apt. . . . So long as we are prepared to face the possibility that, the better some people's mental or physical health, the greater their potentialities for antisocial conduct, we can accept definitions of mental health as an objective neutral condition that is neither determined by, nor necessarily consistent with, any personal or social standards of what constitutes proper or admirable conduct. . . . Most of the current definitions of mental health do not easily lend themselves to such an interpretation. Most of them with their vision of "inner harmonious adjustment", of "trustfulness" and of "socially considerate behaviour"—not to mention happy family life, successful sex adjustment, training for citizenship, economic independence and freedom from industrial unrest—most of them are clearly attempts to formulate conceptions of the ideal, under the guise of healthy man. They express the personal value judgments of their authors rather than scientifically established facts. . . .' Thus the attempt to assimilate mental and physical health and to treat them both alike breaks down. Wootton believes that we have a long way to travel before we can hope to reach an objective, and scientific, definition of mental-cum-physical health which is wholly free of social value judgments, and before we shall be able to treat mental and physical disorders on exactly the same footing. However, the question may also be raised as to whether our journey in this direction is really necessary, or indeed possible. Is not the frank recognition of the part played by assumptions and value judgments, in conjunction with an attempt to identify and measure them, the more fruitful approach in this as in other areas of human endeavour?

Further complicating factors in the demarcation disputes arise over the handling of such phenomena as guilt, responsibility, freedom and choice. These concepts involve profound philosophic and semantic problems. Thus, of guilt Professor McKenzie (1962) writes: 'Both psychiatry and religion are concerned in "making modern man whole". There can be no wholeness without the dissipation of guilt. Can psychiatry offer the forgiveness, the faith, the love, the hope, the insight which according to Jung man needs if he is to be whole? Or must religion and psychiatry co-operate? After all, the Church, unlike the psychotherapist, is not a "new boy" in the "cure of souls". Whatever we may think of theories of Atonement, there can be no question but that the concept of Atonement has brought peace to many a guilt-burdened soul.' Although we may disagree with this interpretation of Jung, we might well agree that, along with the concepts of mental health, guilt *does* imply an 'ought'. Are there things we feel we *should* do and ways we *should* feel, or are moral judgments simply conditioned reflexes, desires, strivings and emotions? There is no 'scientific' answer to this question, and our preference for a physical, psychological or ethico/religious explanation will depend upon our personal assumptions about human nature and the meaning of human existence.

Halmos, in *The Faith of the Counsellors*, has pointed to the movement, in psychotherapy, away from an objective, professional relation with clients to an empathic, committed concern whose essence is 'love', and has argued that this relation may well be the major therapeutic agent. He has argued that, regardless of the deterministic psychological theory professed by the counsellor, underlying his motivation to counsel at all is a protestant Christian ethical attitude to human relations.

Thus 'psychiatrists, lay and medical psychotherapists, clinical psychologists, social caseworkers of several kinds, and some others, have all learnt to share the assumptions and values of the new philanthropic expertise of helping through caring-listening-prompting'. Halmos regards the emergence of this group of 'counsellors' as a new social factor of great influence on the cultural and moral changes in the twentieth-century western society, much as Duverger (1961), in discussing the rise of social science, has described the twentieth century as not only the century of the atom but also the century of social science.

In this insightful study of 'the counsellors', Halmos finds that their tough-minded, scientific assumptions are at variance with their tender-minded therapeutic sympathy and concern, and he finds a scientific, reductionist explanation of the latter unconvincing. 'In his labours the counsellor seems to be guided by an aspiration, by a high-minded conception of what his client might become and should become. By persevering in his efforts to help, the counsellor seems to make a point, take a stand, and declare for hope. At a time when, according to all common-sense standards, the client appears incorrigibly useless, the counsellor is, in fact, saying "You are worth while" and "I am not put off by your illness!" This moral stance of not admitting defeat is possible for those only who have faith or a kind of stubborn confidence in the rightness of what they are doing. Yet all that the counsellors freely confess to is a mere technique, an elaborate professional etiquette, or a sheer casuistry of professional neighbourliness. Just the same, their obvious dedication, persistence, and unthinking affection confess to much more. The literature of counselling is an inspired literature as much as it is a scientific one, and even in their ascetic disowning of inspiration the counsellors testify to an inspired dedication.... This apparently paradoxical stance is actually prescribed for the practitioners of counselling, no matter whether they are psychoanalysts or social caseworkers, clinical psychologists or psychiatrists' (or even, as Halmos argues later on, behaviour therapists). The presuppositions or fundamental faith of the counsellors, often curiously denied or explained away in their literature, include a belief in the counsellor's love as therapeutic skill, the ultimate triumph of love over hatred, the effectiveness of a non-directive therapeutic relationship with clients, and the profound significance of empathy with, and understanding of, the client.

Nor, clearly, can an appeal for more social science provide an escape from the dilemma of underlying value judgments. Although one might argue that physical medicine is closely related to the physical sciences, Heisenberg's much-invoked Principle of Indeterminacy—that one cannot determine accurately both the position and the velocity of a corpuscle at the same time—reminds us that physicists too can be troubled by an interaction between the observer and the observed; and that even in the physical sciences there are no absolute, but only relative, truths. All scientists have preferences and interests which can never be purely scientific, but which may determine the hypotheses and questions to be asked. And the answers obtained may well be preconceived in the formulation of such questions. The choice of question is a product of our valuation (Myrdal 1958). Even in the so-called 'deterministic' sciences, the results of a series of repetitions of the same experiment normally vary within a definite range, and what may be regarded as 'the result' is partly a matter of convention (Frankel 1960). The physical sciences and the social sciences are linked by a major dependence on statistical techniques and probability statements, and by a rejection of strict 'deterministic' explanation.

Psychiatry may be thought of as closer to the social sciences than to the physical in regard to its psychotherapeutic functions and even with regard to diagnosis (Foulds 1965, Rogers 1961). Many therapists have a social science background, and psychiatry's sphere of influence clearly involves areas covered by the behavioural sciences. In his discussion of the relation of value judgments to social inquiry and to the social sciences, Frankel (1960) enumerates six ways in which value judgments may play a part in social scientific endeavour:

1. All social inquirers have preferences, whether acknowledged or not.

2. Such preferences are a part of the initial intuition, ideology, vision or theory with which the social scientist begins his inquiry.
3. Such an initial hypothesis must be present when anyone embarks on a social investigation, since the so-called facts are not immediately observable.
4. Therefore the questions with which social science is concerned have been determined by antecedent value judgments; and, since the conclusions which any social science reaches can only be answers to questions it chooses to ask, a social scientific description is inevitably biased and slanted.
5. It cannot even be assumed that a social science provides us with factual and value-free information about the methods used, since means and ends cannot be sharply differentiated. In psychology, for example, rating scales of certain complex behaviour patterns may be the only available source of measurement, and these may be heavily loaded with value judgments or moral implications.
6. Finally, what is eventually 'proved' by the social sciences depends on the criteria of proof and the evidence that is employed, and these are part and parcel of the original value-loaded 'ideology' with which inquiry began. In addition to these intrinsic difficulties, even at this early stage of development the social sciences require systematic theories in order to be scientifically respectable, and the pressure to select the evidence and interpret the findings of experiments along the lines of some preferred theory is almost irresistible.

Frankel does not accept these arguments in their entirety. He argues, for example, that the fact that social scientists have preferences which influence the inquiry does not distinguish them from natural scientists, and the fact that a question may be biased or contain a value judgment does not imply that the answer is also biased in the sense that another answer is equally possible. Even though a question is slanted, it does not follow that the values which initially impelled it must remain unchanged throughout the course of the subsequent inquiry. The inquirer's original values can be changed by the answers he reaches in the course of his inquiries.

One suspects that this is true only of the more unbiased observers. Bias based on emotional commitment and unconscious motivation is more difficult to shift. Frankel considers that the social sciences have had a limited influence in moulding values because they have not concerned themselves with making factual assertions about the conditions and consequences of the important values that people hold. 'We cannot derive statements of value from statements of fact alone; in this sense the social sciences are "neutral". But assuming that people do have values—which seems a safe assumption—the factual conclusions of the social sciences tend either to challenge or support such values.' Frankel considers that those who attack the belief that social science can aim at a 'detached and immaculate' objectivity are trying to restore a vital connection between theory and practice, and to draw the social sciences into dealing with controversial and therefore important issues rather than to deal with the impartial and therefore inconsequential.

Sorokin (1956) asks whether it is possible to define operationally and study scientifically such all-important phenomena as love and hatred, happiness and despair, Taoism or Christianity or, indeed, any *historical* event. 'A scientist observer who has never experienced joy or sorrow, love or hatred, religious or aesthetic bliss, justice or injustice, creative or dull moments, certitude or doubt, can never obtain even the remotest knowledge of these living, feeling, wishing, emotional and thoughtful states. With all his statistical, logical, observational techniques he can get only shadows of the dead shells of these meaningful, living miracles. He hardly can even count, classify and analyze these phenomena because in order for his countings, classifications, and analyses to be accurate, he must be able to distinguish joy from sorrow, religious ecstasy from sex-drive, love from hatred. If he has never experienced these states, he simply cannot distinguish them from one another and, therefore, cannot classify them into adequate classes and count the identical units in each class.'

Duverger (1961) makes much the same point, and Gershoy (1960) considers that a common situation exists for the scientist, the historian and the artist, since they all must work with a certain artistic and imaginative creativeness, and all their truths are relative and contingent and depend upon 'the working of minds distressingly complex'. May (1958) reminds us that every scientific method rests upon philosophical presuppositions, which determine how much reality an observer with this particular set of spectacles will see, whether what is observed is pertinent to real problems, and whether the scientific work will endure. 'It is a gross, albeit common, error to assume naïvely that one can observe facts best if he avoids all preoccupations with philosophical assumptions. All he does, then, is to mirror uncritically the particular parochial doctrines of his own limited culture.... It seems especially a misfortune that our understanding in such a crucial area as the psychological study of man, with the understanding of emotional and mental health depending upon it, should be curtailed by uncritical acceptance of limited assumptions.... The only way to widen one's "blinders" is to analyze one's philosophical assumptions.'

In the critical literature on the present status of the social sciences in this post-Freudian/Einsteinian era views such as these are commonly expressed. What is important, however, as Frankel (1960) points out, is not that we operate on assumptions and values, but that the issue should not be dodged. The acceptance of personal assumptions and presuppositions as a basis of action and decision is the general orientation of this book; and in the section describing our research an attempt will be made to determine the personal assumptions concerning treatment of a number of occupational groups working in the psychiatric field and, where possible within the limits of this study, to assess the effect of these assumptions on the patients.

CHAPTER 2

Basic assumptions of the psychiatric schools

In this chapter a number of orientations to the treatment of mental illness will be considered from the point of view of the assumptions that they involve. We shall pay particular attention to the methods which are most commonly used in National Health Service hospitals in this country.

For the purpose of our argument, treatment orientations or theories can in general be split into two main strands: those which claim, usually aggressively, to rest on firmly scientific foundations, and those which stem more from religious or philosophical traditions. The first are concerned with causes and explanations in a broadly mechanistic framework, with little explicit reference to values. They are retrospective rather than teleological; and explanations may gain primacy over ends to the extent that demonstration of a pathological cause for a particular type of behaviour negates any value that that behaviour may have in itself (William James called this 'medical materialism'). This kind of approach tends to equate science with mechanistic explanation, the underlying fear seeming to be that since the phenomena of mental illness have no obvious cause and effect quality, a further, usually biological mechanism must be found to account for them. Systems of psychotherapy derived from philosophic-religious traditions are usually more concerned with goals, aims and values, intentions rather than explanations. Less stress is laid on the scientific nature of such theories, which tend to be more overtly concerned with value judgments and with the meaning and purpose of psychopathological experience.

This distinction is inevitably a little artificial; but, while in practice it may be difficult to draw a strictly accurate line of demarcation between the two types of theory, it may help to provide a framework for the arguments to be presented below.

In the first of these categories (the 'scientific' orientations) we find the methods of treatment most widely practiced in mental hospitals in this country—organic psychiatry, psychoanalytically oriented psychotherapy, and behaviour therapy, this last being a much more recent addition which will not be discussed in any great detail here. In theory these are clearly distinguishable from each other; and, indeed, many people will feel surprised at seeing them bracketed together in this way, since in the past there has been a good deal of acrimonious dispute between the so-called 'organic' psychiatrists and their 'dynamic' psychoanalytic colleagues. In practice, distinctions are not always easy to make, since relatively few proponents of a single discipline exist in pure culture, and probably the majority of psychiatrists would call themselves eclectic—faced with the bewildering and disturbing suffering of the mentally ill, the doctor may feel he must use whatever method might work under the circumstances, and in this he will be guided as much by current fashion as by ideological principles. However, there are fairly basic factors which these approaches do tend to share, despite appearances to the contrary. To begin with, they share the value judgment that only mechanistic-scientific explanations can be of use in understanding mental illness. They also have a good deal in common in terms of the type of relationship which is allowed, or encouraged, between doctor and patient. This is very much one of the expert who is equipped with a body of specialized knowledge not available to the layman performing certain operations on the patient, who must take his treatment on trust. Real social interaction between the two, on a level at which both are equal, is unnecessary; indeed, it would be a complicating factor and should be discouraged.

Thus the organic psychiatrist, apart from needing to gain sufficient *rapport* with his patient to enable meaningful and relatively uninhibited communication to pass between them—enough to establish what symptoms the patient is suffering from—would find any kind of deeper involvement disruptive of his function as purveyor of medicines, drugs, electro-convulsive therapy, brain surgery, etc. The patient is basically a disordered organism in need of mechanical readjustment. 'The patient expects the doctor to have the same scientific detached attitude towards his emotional problems as he has towards his physical complaints, and psychology provides an objective standpoint from which the doctor can be helped to achieve the sophistication expected of him' (Mowbray and Rodger 1963, p. 5).

The behaviour therapist applies a standard technique in retraining the habitual, maladaptive responses of his patient, in which his own personality is held to be of only secondary importance, if at all. The psychoanalyst arranges matters in such a manner that he may gain a view of the patient's disordered early relationships, focused on the well-known oral, anal and genital stages of development, and acquire an appreciation of the ways in which the primary drives of sexuality and aggression are functioning. To do this he also maintains a relatively impersonal role, taking care that his own emotional and intellectual responses do not 'interfere' with those of his patient. It is true that *vis-à-vis* the patient he plays a very important role ('transference'), but in this he tends to be passive, a receptacle for projections. Chertok (1966) conceives of the relationship in these terms: 'For the relationship to develop in the most advantageous way, the psychoanalyst keeps a certain degree of distance between himself and the patient, and assumes a neutral attitude.'

There are unquestionably many practitioners of these techniques, particularly among psychoanalysts, who would claim that some more direct kind of involvement with patients would be desirable; but though we are inevitably oversimplifying matters, we would feel that we have given a not too misleading impression of the kind of therapist–patient relationship most frequently fostered by exponents of the techniques under discussion. In *The Faith of the Counsellors* Halmos (1965) is concerned to show that, particularly in the case of psychoanalysis, the relationship, at least on the part of the therapist, is basically one of selfless love; and he provides an impressive documentation of this view from many sources. However, he does indicate (p. 122) that such confessions of faith tend to be 'made at the end of a working day which had seemed to consist of ratiocination alone', and we should maintain that the average psychiatrist would, as far as his patients would be able to see, place more emphasis on the scientific, detached nature of his relationship to the patient. The reason often advanced for this is that, should any more direct kind of relationship be entered into, the psychiatrist, or psychoanalyst, would be using the patient for his own pathological ends. This would seem to involve the curious view that the therapist is incapable of having any kind of relationship with people that is neither detached nor pathological.

One of the most outspoken critics of this aspect of the psychotherapeutic relationship is S. M. Jourard. The following quotations are taken from his book *The Transparent Self* (Jourard 1964). '*Effective* therapists seem to follow this implicit hypothesis: if they *are themselves* in the presence of the patient, avoiding *compulsions* to silence, to reflection, to interpretation, to impersonal technique, and kindred character disorders, but instead striving to know their patient, involving themselves in his situation, and then responding to his utterances with their spontaneous selves, this fosters growth' (p. 62). Again: 'Just as a patient will pick and choose his utterances for their intended effect on the therapist (a violation of Freud's fundamental rule), so will a therapist often pick and choose his behaviour for its supposed effect on the patient. This I now see as a violation of what may become a fundamental rule for the therapist: that he should be spontaneously open in response to the patient. Resistance to being, to being oneself with the patient, seems to be quite as characteristic of beginning therapists and of more experienced "technicians" of therapy as it is of patients, and often for similar reasons, e.g. latent fear of how one will seem to the other as well as how one will seem to oneself, or dread of what will happen if one "let's go" of one's tight self-control' (p. 66). Of the view that technique is necessary in order for the therapist to avoid having a pathological relationship with his patient, Jourard has this to say (p. 71): 'I don't think expert technique can long hide immaturity, anxiety, hostility, sexuality, if these exist in the therapist. Patients are seldom that insensitive. Moreover, if a therapist thus hides his being, he is engaging in the same behaviour that generated symptoms in the patient, and, supposedly, he is trying to undo this self-alienating process.'

The theme of the therapist–patient relationship is one to which we shall return many times in this book, and we should come back now to a more detailed consideration of the assumptions which underly the 'scientific' orientations to treatment described above.

The main conflict between these three orientations lies at the point at which each adopts its basic assumptions. A basic assumption might be defined as one which delineates an area of investigation and limits the type of evidence which will be considered relevant and admissible to the theory. One might argue that the more constricting the basic assumption, the less the theory can be considered scientific. Thus one suspects that orientations in psychiatry which lay claim to being scientific, and at the same time rest on a rigid set of assumptions, do so on the basis more of their having acquired the trappings and surface technology of science than of their having sifted as objectively as possible all the data available on the phenomena of mental illness. This is betrayed, for example, in the behaviour therapist's insistence that there is nothing 'underlying' the symptoms of neurosis (e.g. Eysenck 1959). Having made the highly constricting assumption that a neurosis can be nothing more than its symptoms, no amount of evidence to the contrary would be admissible, since it has been made logically impossible. This does not seem to be a scientific procedure. The behaviour therapists' claim to scientific respectability rests on their having borrowed from experimental psychology the methods and jargon developed in learning theory (which is built mainly on experiments with animals, and rests on the philosophy of behaviourism, which Koch, 1964, has called 'a deep metaphysical bias') and applied it to the development of psychopathology in man. While the scientific understanding of learning which experimental psychologists have gained with rats and pigeons may have far-reaching value, its uncritical application to the mentally ill seems to us a dangerous step if accepted on the grounds of scientific demonstration, since there is no scientific reason to assume that rats and pigeons are in any important or relevant way similar to the mentally ill. Again, that the behaviour therapist, in his attempt to 'extinguish' neurotic behaviour in human patients, tends to resort to the use of electric shock machines and other paraphernalia (admittedly necessary for conveying our purpose to animals) seems to reflect an almost ludicrous indifference to one of the foremost distinguishing features of man, namely that he has the ability to use language. The 'laws of learning' function adequately as explanations only in the greatly simplified setting of the animal laboratory, and concepts basic to conditioning theories are *dictated by* the experimental conditions rather than *inferred from* the animal's behaviour: to induce an animal to perform an artificial task of our own choosing, it is clearly necessary to 'motivate' it by, say, depriving it of food ('hunger drive') so that it will 'respond' by seeking the reward of food ('reinforcement'). Moreover, the variability of behaviour possible for a rat in, for example, an experimental maze, is greatly limited. Thus it would be hard enough to account for the behaviour of an animal *outside* the experimental (laboratory) situation, let alone a human being.

These are points which have been laboured by many writers in recent years, and need not concern us further. It should be noted, however, that not all behaviourists who have addressed themselves to the problems involved in psychotherapy have demonstrated quite as much dogmatism and lack of self-criticism as some of the more recent accounts (e.g. Wolpe *et al.* 1964) might suggest. An early attempt to *reconcile* learning theory with psychoanalysis (rather than to oppose it as 'unscientific') was that of Dollard and Miller (1950). Again, some modern practitioners of behaviour therapy (e.g. Marks and Gelder 1966) show an acute awareness of the problems involved, and resist the temptation to oversimplification of theory and exaggeration of claims otherwise widely evident in proponents of this discipline.

Many behaviour therapists also claim the authority of science for their views, in that they employ respectable statistical methods in the evaluation of the success of this method of treatment. This raises questions which will be considered later; it need only be noted here that scientific evaluation of the results of a method of treatment does not mean that the method itself has been developed along scientific principles.

The main basic assumption of the organic psychiatrist is that there must be a physical cause for mental disturbance. The proper fields for inquiry are therefore genetic, physiological and biochemical. This leads to a great deal of time and energy being spent on combing through areas felt to be relevant, with too little thought being given to how relevant they really are. Thus there is a quite massive literature on the physical basis of schizophrenia, with patients suffering from this illness having been examined from every conceivable medical point of view (see Bellak 1958, Jackson 1960). So far no consistent positive findings have emerged, despite euphoric predictions that the end is in sight appearing with fair regularity in scientific journals, the press and television. The adherents of this belief often seem to subscribe to the 'pack of cards' view of inductive reasoning, in which the more often you do not find something, the more likely it becomes that it will turn up in the next thing you examine. This is to some extent exemplified in the following quotation (Fish 1966): 'Until we can classify mental illness according to underlying neurophysiological and biochemical changes, we can add nothing new to the arguments about the concepts of schizophrenia and dementia praecox, which have occupied the best minds of psychiatry for the last seventy years.' Again with schizophrenia, the proposition that the disease is determined in part genetically is accepted by nearly all psychiatrists almost without question. It could be maintained that this acceptance is guided more by the 'medical assumption' than by scientific evidence, since quite profound difficulties have been shown to exist with this view. It is certainly not enough to show that schizophrenia—or any other functional mental illness—'runs in families'; one can think of many behavioural phenomena which may typify membership of a given family and yet which clearly depend on processes of social learning rather than on genetic inheritance—for instance, habits of language or speech. Without being able to demonstrate some kind of clearly hereditary physical characteristic underlying schizophrenia, the research worker is ultimately forced to rely on the complex analysis of family incidence of 'disease', in which the study of identical twins separated at birth and raised apart plays a major role. Quite apart from such difficulties as establishing (often retrospectively) diagnoses satisfactorily, the frequency of cases of identical twins fulfilling these conditions is too limited to provide convincing evidence. These and other criticisms of the arguments for the hereditary basis of schizophrenia may be found in, for example, Jackson (1960) and Tienari (1963).

Laing (1967, p. 99) has written of schizophrenia: 'It is easy to forget that the process is a hypothesis, to assume that it is a fact, then to pass the judgment that it is biologically maladaptive and, as such, pathological.' To assume further that the pathological process must be traceable to some physiological cause has no justification in science.

Many people now feel that the ingenuity shown in the past in defining and identifying syndromes of mental illness could usefully be applied to reconsidering the necessity for such an approach at all. Eysenck (1960, ch. 1) has argued that the disease entity model of what we call mental illness has outlived its usefulness, but one can appreciate that the basic assumptions of organic psychiatry would alone be enough to ensure its stubborn adherence to the threads of life. Thus in organic psychiatry, phenomenology is secondary to diagnosis, though it is open to question whether diagnostic judgments—'biological value judgments', as Binswanger (1958, p. 330) calls them—are any more basic than the phenomena they supposedly give rise to.

The organic psychiatrist's methods of treatment are loosely empirical rather than founded on theory (in contrast to the other two treatment orientations under discussion), or indeed on scientific fact. The indications for the use of drugs, electrical treatment or leucotomy are to be found in the textbooks of psychiatry, and are handed down by authority. The scientific basis for their use is poor, and though evidence for a given technique is often cited, it is often one-sided and could easily be matched with contradictory evidence. Methods of treatment are dictated, as has already been indicated, largely by fashion. Anything which is felt likely to work is tried—Campbell's (1960) review of the literature on electro-convulsive therapy would suggest that evidence for the usefulness of even this psychiatric standby is far from conclusive.

The kind of strategy adopted by medical (and other) research workers in the field of psychiatry is often naïvely oversimplified, based as it frequently is on a crudely mechanistic view of the human psyche. Thus, in a rather cursory search for 'psychological factors' in, for example, schizophrenia, research workers will often be content to examine hastily written case notes for evidence of common features in patients' backgrounds, or will count the incidence of such specific factors as 'broken homes' or 'death of a parent'. Here we may agree with Kind (1966), who writes: 'The most serious objection is that these investigations are based on the unlikely expectation that single defined misfortunes or psychic traumata are particularly apt to bring about the faulty development which ends in schizophrenia. Discovering a broken home tells one nothing about the significance of such an event for a schizophrenic's life history; still less can the absence of such misfortunes imply that the patient grew up in a normal family environment.'

One can only sympathize with the psychiatrist: he is faced with a practical task, and if he is forced to rely on belief rather than knowledge, one cannot blame him—belief is the only alternative to paralysis in the face of our lack of conclusive scientific evidence. If he turns to the scientific literature, he is faced with a sea of contradictions. However, not the least of the organic psychiatrist's difficulties is his acceptance of the biological-medical basic assumption. In this context we may again cite the views of Binswanger (1958, p. 331): '... we are dealing here with a tremendous oversimplification, reinterpretation and reduction of human existence down to the categories of natural science. All this, however, psychopathology accepts in order to find that "connection" with biology which, as noted, alone warrants the concept of illness in the medical sense and the possibility of a medical diagnosis and a causal therapy.' Again in the context of schizophrenia, Kind's (1966) article lends further support to our general argument: 'What needs pointing out, however—and this becomes very evident to anyone who examines the history of the investigation of schizophrenia at all closely—is that so many of the aetiological theories derive in the first place from fundamental convictions which influence the worker's choice of observations and the observations themselves; it is far less common to find unprejudiced observations leading to the formulation of theories.' And of the views of perhaps the most influential of the founders of organic psychiatry Kind states: 'It is evident that Kraepelin's views on aetiology were guided far more by his general principles and convictions—corresponding as they did to the then prevailing tendencies of medicine to base itself exclusively on the natural sciences—than by any unprejudiced assessment of the available facts.'

The underlying assumption of the psychoanalytic school, based ultimately on Freud's observations of his patients, is that the personality and pathology of the individual are established in the early years of childhood, and revolve round conflicts experienced over sexuality and aggression. All later behavioural phenomena are considered to rest on this foundation. The fact that psychoanalysts tend to focus on these areas to the exclusion of others, and have developed a set of theoretical entities (defence mechanisms, etc.) which can be made to account for any variations in behaviour in these terms, makes the general body of theory difficult (though not necessarily impossible) to test in any way which cannot be made self fulfilling. Moreover, many psychoanalysts tend to eschew what they consider to be limiting and data-distorting quantification of theory of a kind which would make it possible to perform scientific experiments on their theories. Here again it seems to be more that the trappings and techniques of science are important rather than the sound application of truly scientific methods. Freud, in common with other important figures of his time, had an almost touching belief in rationality, and the main claim of psychoanalysis to being scientific seems to rest on the certainty of there being relatively simple rational explanations for behaviour, as well as on the fact that the discipline has a medical background (though Freud laid a good deal less stress on this as a qualification for analysts than most of his colleagues); these are, however, more matters of appearance than convincing demonstrations of a really scientific approach. Freud's equation of science with reason is illustrated in the following quotation (Freud 1949, p. 219): 'Our best hope for the future is that the intellect—the scientific spirit, reason—should in time establish a dictatorship over the human mind.' That the insights of philosophy, art or religion could be of value in our understanding of man and the world is emphatically denied by Freud (op. cit., p. 205): 'The bare fact is that truth cannot be tolerant and cannot admit compromise or limitations, that scientific research looks on the whole field of human activity as its own, and must adopt an uncompromisingly critical attitude towards any other power that seeks to usurp any part of its province.'

Criticisms of psychoanalysis and its effectiveness as a method of treatment are well known, and it would be impossible in this chapter to try to carry out anything like an adequate review of the arguments for and against these views. The point to be made is that psychoanalysis is guided by a relatively narrow set of assumptions based on a mechanistic nineteenth-century philosophy, and though claiming to be a scientific discipline, does not in fact easily permit scientific examination of the validity of its basic postulates—as Freud himself stated (op. cit., p. 223): '. . . the analyst is unlike other scientific workers in this one respect, that he has to do without the help that experiment can bring to research'. It may be true that Freud arrived at his formulations of theory on the basis of empirical experience with patients, and no doubt this sort of activity forms a necessary part of any scientific venture. It does however, seem doubtful whether such activity can by itself justify the claim that psychoanalysis is a scientific discipline.

The point we wish to make is that none of the methods of treatment for the mentally ill which have been discussed so far in this chapter can justify the claim often made for them that they are based purely on scientific inquiry, although they undoubtedly contain elements of scientific method and many of the appearances of science. This is not to say that such methods are of no value, nor that only a truly scientific method could be of value—our aim at this point is to understand the attitudes behind the theories, not to pass judgment on their effectiveness. The importance of understanding basic attitudes and assumptions does not lie in discovering contradictions and thus attempting to discredit the usefulness of the theories which they underpin, but rather in tracing the effects such assumptions have on the way in which a method of treatment is carried out, and the meaning of this for the patient. Thus, in the cases discussed so far, the patient is led to believe that he is being treated by methods which are grounded on scientific fact. Whether the fact that this is not true has any important repercussions remains to be seen. It does have definite implications for the type of relationship that is built up between doctor and patient, and this appears to us to be one of the more important aspects of the problem, which we shall clarify in later chapters.

We also wish to avoid giving the impression that the theories of treatment under discussion have made no contribution to the scientific understanding and examination of human psychology and pathology—the scientific literature is full of experiments and hypotheses derived from them, and indeed most scientific investigations in this field lean heavily on one or other of these approaches. The point is that so far there is virtually nothing in the way of *established fact* which could justifiably lead to the claim that the processes of treatment based on these orientations have a scientifically established foundation. They are, in fact, founded on assumption and faith; this need not in itself be deleterious, as long as it is recognized. Halmos (1965, p. 106) provides a convenient summary of our argument where, in his consideration of psychotherapeutic counselling, he says: 'The trouble is that the very concept of an "applied socio-psychological science" is somewhat blurred at the edges. At the centre, where things are sharper, we may observe that an "applied science" is a system of theoretical generalizations about certain tools and procedures which can be used to modify part of our universe. The essential point is that in the various "technologies", for example, in engineering or medicine, the theoretical generalizations are usually verified before they lead to the construction and use of tools, or to the manipulation of substances, whereas in counselling, the theoretical generalizations often lead straight to action, even when they have not been verified. Or in other words, in the technologies there is no doubt that what we apply is *science*, whilst in counselling there is a great deal of doubt.' One can, of course, argue that Halmos overstates his case here, and that one of the distinguishing features of 'technology', compared with 'pure' science, is the very fact that in the former techniques found to 'work' are frequently put to practical application before they have received any theoretical justification (see, for example,

Polanyi 1958). Nevertheless, his point is probably valid if one contrasts the *degree* to which applied social science and applied natural science rest on well (scientifically) established foundations.

If psychiatrists, psychoanalysts and behaviour therapists were truly to rely on the establishment of a firm, scientific, factual basis for their treatment of the mentally ill, they would not yet have attempted to treat a single patient (of those held to be suffering from 'functional' mental illness), since no such body of knowledge exists. Practically any theory can claim to be scientific if by this all that is meant is that one has observed the phenomena of illness, gained some ideas about their nature and cause, and developed hypotheses which might in principle be subject to some kind of experimental test. Indeed, this contains some of the ingredients of science, and we should have little quarrel with such an approach. It is only when such a claim is made as a *justification* for a method of treatment, as against competing methods, that it becomes necessary to point out the consequent fallacy that somehow that method has a greater right to be accepted. Quite apart from the fact that the types of basic assumption noted in the methods under discussion limit the kind of scientific evidence which is logically relevant to a theory, and even given scientifically established psychological knowledge, the development of a therapeutic system based upon it involves quite obvious value judgments about what is 'good' for people. Freud himself seems to have been in some confusion on this point (1949, p. 207), since although he claims that 'science is content with discussing and stating facts', he nevertheless feels that 'it is true that from the applications of science rules and recommendations for behaviour may be deduced'. Despite its being a well-known philosophical impossibility, Freud is certainly not alone in feeling that an 'ought' can be derived from an 'is'; the psychologist Maslow (1962) in his enthusiastic inquiry into applying the methods of science as a short route to mystical experience, also seems to feel that a blueprint for living could be arrived at by studying and emulating the healthiest, most creative (note the implicit value judgment) members of society. Value judgments are inevitable and they should be accepted openly, not smuggled in under the guise of science.

Theories of psychology and psychological treatment resting on the philosophic-religious tradition are many and varied. Their main common feature is the emphasis laid on the purposive nature of man's behaviour (and psychopathology) in relation to his moral and existential problems. Proponents of these views would probably not relish the charge of being unscientific (nor would such a charge be any more or less justified than with the orientations already discussed), but they would perhaps be less interested in insisting on a scientific basis to their work as though this gave it a special claim to respectability. Since proponents of these schools are only infrequently met with in mental hospitals in this country, we shall limit ourselves to a consideration of two or three examples chosen more or less at random.

Jungian analytical psychology is probably the first major discipline which springs to mind when considering psychological theories of this type. Although Jung, in what he called his 'scientific' works, emphasized the empirical evidence for his views, he saw that this need not restrict him to the kind of reductive and 'nothing but' psychology of Freudian psychoanalysis, and felt that 'the human psyche is far more than a mere object of scientific interest' (Jung 1954, p. 75). He felt the search for religious meaning and satisfaction to be man's central problem, especially in the second half of life. Though he insisted on the medical nature of psychotherapy, one does not gain an impression of Jung as a medical man, but more as a scholar, anthropologist, philosopher, and even theologian. His scientific conscience forbade him to make claims for his views on any but empirical grounds, although it is clear from his letters (for example, White 1952) and from his 'autobiography' (Jung 1963) (that he had very definite religious beliefs, which carried great weight in his private life. His care to give some sort of evidence for his views in his 'scientific' works (even if it is evidence not acceptable to the experimental scientist) invalidates the charge of mysticism so frequently levelled against him by those who presumably find his reasoning in general mysterious and respect only the early work he did on word association (which was, in fact, quite insignificant in the context of his later output). It is, however, clear from *Memories, Dreams and Reflections* (Jung 1963) that Jung did in fact undergo mystical experiences (some may prefer 'psychotic interludes'), which must profoundly have influenced his attitude to his work. His main point of difference from Freud is that he regarded mental illness for the most part as a striving towards integration and understanding of the purposive and essentially religious nature of man's life, rather than as the disordered expression of infantile frustrations, although he did not fail to take account of the latter. Jung's concern with the meaning of religious symbolism and the problem of man's relatedness to himself which he felt it to reflect led to a more complex theoretical structure than that of Freud, in terms both of the data to be considered relevant in their own right, and of the amount of uncertainty to be tolerated by the system. Thus Jung maintains (1954, p. 5): 'If I wish to treat another individual psychologically at all, I must for better or worse give up all pretensions to superior knowledge, all authority and desire to influence. I must perforce adopt a dialectical procedure consisting in a comparison of our mutual findings.' His tolerance of uncertainty is again evident in the following quotation (op. cit., p. 71): 'It is enough to drive me to despair that in practical psychology there are no universally valid recipes and rules. There are only individual cases with the most heterogeneous needs and demands—so heterogeneous that we can virtually never know in advance what course a given case will take, for which reason it is better for the doctor to abandon all preconceived opinions. This does not mean that he should throw them overboard, but that in any given case he should use them merely as hypotheses for a possible explanation.'

This greater tolerance of uncertainty and emphasis on the individuality of the patient leads to a different kind of relationship between doctor and patient from that in Freudian analysis and psychiatry: 'The touchstone of every analysis that has not stopped short at partial success, or come to a standstill with no success at all, is always the person-to-person relationship, a psychological situation where the patient confronts the doctor upon equal terms, and with the same ruthless criticism that he must inevitably learn from the doctor in the course of his treatment' (op. cit., p. 137). Again, Jung feels that 'it is not the doctor's whole task to instruct or convince his patient; but rather to show how the doctor reacts to that particular individual. For, twist and turn the matter as we may, the relation between doctor and patient remains a personal one within the impersonal framework of professional treatment. By no device can the treatment be anything but the product of mutual influence, in which the whole being of the doctor as well as that of his patient plays its part. . . . For two personalities to meet is like mixing two different chemical substances: if there is any combination at all, both are transformed. In any effective psychological treatment the doctor is bound to influence the patient; but this influence can only take place if the patient has a reciprocal influence on the doctor. You can exert no influence if you are not susceptible to influence. It is futile for the doctor to shield himself from the influence of the patient and to surround himself with a smoke-screen of fatherly and professional authority. By so doing he only denies himself the use of a highly important organ of information. The patient influences him unconsciously none the less' (op. cit., p. 71).

The scope and breadth of Jung's work is enormous, and no attempt can be made here to present anything like an adequate consideration of it. His deep concern with religious experience and symbolism may be contrasted with the simplicity with which Freud, with his faith in rationalism and his distaste for value judgments, could dismiss the problem of religion, for example, in *The Future of an Illusion* (Freud 1928). 'Medical materialism' of the kind exemplified by Freud's work in this connexion may have no horrors for some, and the arguments for and against such an approach are at the present state of our knowledge no more than persuasive. There are few external criteria which allow one to choose between the acceptability of one man's interpretation of his empirical observations as against that of another. The more diverse the data which may be considered relevant to a theory, perhaps, the greater is the chance of finding data which are in fact relevant to scientific understanding. Otherwise, choice between approaches can only be a matter of personal preference and values.

Jung's concern with the connexions between psychology and religion received (somewhat uneasy) support and interest from some of those more firmly entrenched in the clerical camp, in particular the Catholic theologian Victor White. However, the conflict between psychological observation and religious dogma led to the rejection of some of Jung's most central arguments (for instance, concerning the 'problem of evil', in which Jung took the position that evil consisted in something very much more real than a mere *privatio boni*), and the hopelessness of achieving a fruitful marriage between the two disciplines is particularly evident in White's book *Soul and Psyche* (1960), where there is a noticeable cooling of the enthusiasm he displayed in his earlier work *God and the Unconscious* (1952). It is clear that one could hardly expect orthodox Christians to be able to accept the view that God is destructive and vengeful as well as good and loving. Although this degree of cross-fertilization may demonstrate that here is a field common both to the Church and to medical psychology in many aspects, it seems probable that the interchange between psychology and religion, if it is to bear fruit, will have to be carried on outside the inner core either of the medical profession or of the Church, since the basic assumptions of these would almost certainly prove too constricting.

A very much more recent theory concerning the connexions between psychopathology, psychotherapy and religion is that of O. H. Mowrer. In comparison with Jung's system it is simple and specific, standing in relation to it as a Baptist chapel to a Gothic cathedral. However, it is not our intention to compare the two here, but rather to present another example.

Mowrer started out as a more or less orthodox behavioural psychologist, and is best known in Britain for his activities in this sphere; but it is with his views on psychopathology that we shall be concerned here. In his book *The Crisis in Psychiatry and Religion* (1961), Mowrer draws attention to the present-day need for, and lack of, a real morality and system of values. Clerical apathy has allowed the treatment of mental disorder to end up in medical hands, though, he suggests, the medical profession is quite unsuited to coping with problems which are essentially moral. His main theme is to stress the reality of sin and guilt and the central part which these play in the formation of psychopathology. The sufferer from mental illness, Mowrer thinks, is troubled by past actions of his which are, if only in his own eyes, morally wrong, rather than by impulses which he would like to act out, but is afraid to (which would be more the traditional psychoanalytic position). Thus for Mowrer it is the superego, or conscience, rather than the id which is repressed. Unlike the psychoanalysts, Mowrer feels that the conscience cannot be too strong, even though the reality of sin is subjective and relative; and in this context he likens the activities of psychoanalysts to those of the devil, inasmuch as they tempt the individual away from the dictates of his conscience. In Mowrer's view, the principal curative measures are confession and restitution. Neurotic individuals, he suggests, are morally responsible for their state of sin, and psychoanalysis exploits rather than treats the problem; he prefers the therapeutic approach adopted by such organizations as Alcoholics Anonymous and the Salvation Army! In particular, it is the secrecy of sin which he feels is punishing, and confession must be publicly carried out to the 'significant others' in the patient's life. These really are the basic assumptions behind Mowrer's views, and though he offers empirical evidence (of a kind) for them, that evidence is no more or less convincing than that offered by other theorists. His answers are relatively simple, and in this sense approach the kinds of reductive explanation offered in the 'scientific' disciplines discussed earlier. In fact, he has little use for the concept of self-knowledge, seeing guilt as an interpersonal and social problem. In total opposition to Jung, he has no respect for what he considers to be the 'ethical nihilism' of the 'anti-intellectual' religions of the East.

In recent years some psychotherapists and psychiatrists have become very much preoccupied with the implications for their discipline of the philosophical movement known broadly as 'existentialism', as it is represented by the views of such diverse proponents as Kierkegaard, Heidegger, Buber, Tillich and Sartre. Here the concern is with the function and meaning of mental illness to the sufferer, not as the automatic behavioural expression of a disordered organism, but as the direct expression of the patient's immediate ontological predicament. This has led to systems in psychiatry such as existential analysis (*Daseinsanalyse*)—represented in particular by Ludwig Binswanger—and, in Britain, to R. D. Laing's views on the nature and treatment of schizophrenia. The existentialist movement has also had considerable impact on more recent systems of psychotherapy such as that developed by Carl Rogers.

A review of the scope and significance of this movement in psychiatry would be out of place here, and the reader will find an adequate treatment of it in May *et al.* (1958). Of particular interest for present purposes are the implications of this kind of approach for the way in which the therapist approaches his patient and the relationship he has with him. Thus the attempt is not to be guided by a set of theoretical assumptions, but by the significance of the immediate therapeutic encounter; and this necessitates the therapist playing in many respects as active a part as his patient. The central effort is away from reductionism, as it is felt that the individual in this case is likely to be obscured by an emphasis on mechanisms. Proponents of this school see no particular virtue in so-called 'scientific objectivity', which, in the study of human beings, can only be depersonalizing. To look upon a person as an organism splits up reality, and should not be confused with the person himself. As Laing points out (1960), 'To see "signs" of "disease" is not to see neutrally. Nor is it neutral to see a smile as contractions of the circumoral muscles.' The implications of this kind of approach for the therapist–patient relationship are outlined by May (1958, p. 38): 'The encounter with the being of another person has the power to shake one profoundly and may potentially be very anxiety-arousing. It may also be joy-creating. In either case, it has the power to grasp and move one deeply. The therapist may understandably be tempted for his own comfort to abstract himself from the encounter by thinking of the other just as a "patient", or by focusing only on certain mechanisms of behaviour. But if the technical view is used dominantly in the relating to the other person, obviously one has defended himself from anxiety at the price not only of the isolation of himself from the other but also of radical distortion of reality. For one does not then really *see* the other person.'

Of the 'scientific' aspect of the existential approach, May (op.

cit., p. 8) has this to say: 'It is well to remember that the existential movement in psychiatry and psychology arose precisely out of a passion to be not *less* but *more* empirical. Binswanger and the others were convinced that the traditional scientific methods not only did not do justice to the data, but actually tended to hide rather than reveal what was going on in the patient. The existential analysis movement is a protest against the tendency to see the patient in forms tailored to our own preconceptions or to make him over into the image of our own predilections. In this respect it stands squarely within the scientific tradition in its widest sense.'

Binswanger (1958, p. 315) emphasizes the greater flexibility of existential analysis, compared with orthodox psychoanalysis, in the following terms: 'Since existential analysis undertakes to work out being-human in all its existential forms and their worlds, in its being-able-to-be (existence), being-allowed-to-be (love), and having-to-be (thrownness), whereas psychoanalysis does so only in respect to the last of these, it is clear that existential analysis is able to widen and deepen the basic concepts and understandings of psychoanalysis. Psychoanalysis, on the other hand, can only constrict and flatten the existential-analytic forms, that is, reduce them to the plane of its (one-sidedly naturalistic-evolutionary) viewpoint.' Binswanger makes it clear in this context that for him, unlike Freud, phenomenology takes precedence over postulated mechanisms such as orality and anality. *Daseinsanalyse* opposes any attempt to explanation as such, the idea being rather to understand, for example, anal and oral *phenomena* as the expression of the individual's organization of his world.

To those brought up in the tradition of British empiricism, the language in which existentialists often couch their philosophical and psychological insights frequently seems unnecessarily obscure, sometimes to the extent that their specialized vocabulary can only be understood, presumably, by a chosen few. The following quotation from the beginning of Kierkegaard's *The Sickness unto Death* (1955, p. 146) may be used to illustrate this point: 'Man is spirit. But what is spirit? Spirit is the self. But what is the self? The self is a relation which relates itself to its own self, or it is that in the relation [which accounts for it] that the relation relates itself to its own self; the self is not the relation but [consists in the fact] that the relation relates itself to its own self. Man is a synthesis of the infinite and the finite, of the temporal and the eternal, of freedom and necessity, in short it is a synthesis. A synthesis is a relation between two factors. So regarded, man is not yet a self.' To ears attuned to the strains of Locke and Hume, not to mention logical positivism, this may seem little more than meaningless metaphysical nonsense; and one cannot help agreeing with Koch (1964) that existential writers often seem to have 'a high tolerance, if not a positive appetite, for the opaque'. And yet in the work of existential analysts and phenomenologists such apparently impossibly abstruse ideas as these have led to concrete courses of action of considerable significance for the treatment of the mentally ill.

Our aim in this chapter has not been to present a review of all the psychological theories relevant to the field of mental illness, nor do we pretend to have discussed necessarily the most important contributions to knowledge in this area—the reader will be familiar with many well-known names, particularly among the more notable deviants from the orthodox psychoanalytic line, which have received no mention. Our concern has been rather to provide a basis for our argument that no system of psychological treatment exists which has been derived from anything scientifically more sound than assumption and hypothesis, and we do not believe that we have failed to mention any system of which this is not true.

Our own preferences and biases concerning the methods of treatment for mental illness discussed above should by now be quite obvious, and it would be futile to pretend that we are not as prone to the influence of basic assumptions as any other worker in this field. Our plea is only that assumptions and value systems should be acknowledged and made explicit, since, as things stand, no more rational basis of the theory and practice of treatment is possible. Thus our sympathy inclines more towards those theories which openly admit that they are guided by value systems which have in the last analysis little to do with an objectivist conception of science, and which do not strive too hard in the name of science to force the phenomena of illness into reductive, mechanistic moulds.

CHAPTER 3

The therapeutic community

The previous chapters have dealt in a general way with the underlying assumptions associated with certain treatment orientations and procedures. The remainder of the book will be concerned more specifically with therapeutic communities, with the assessment of one such community as a therapeutic technique, and with what seem to us to be some of the implications of research for the practice of psychiatry and for psychiatric nursing.

The conscious employment of community social processes for the psychotherapy of mentally ill patients is frequently referred to as a 'revolution' in psychiatry (Dreikurs 1955, Moreno 1952, Rapoport 1960). The first two revolutions have been described by Zilboorg and Henry (1941), who have related changes in psychiatric ideas and practice to the more general evolution in thought taking place in western society as a whole (see also chapter 1). Thus the first psychiatric revolution, culminating in the sixteenth century, formed a part of the general emancipation of scientific from theological thought and presuppositions, and was accomplished through the scholarly rather than the medical tradition by such humanitarians as Giordano Bruno, Francis Bacon, Thomas More, Erasmus and particularly Juan Vives. The revolution in thought and belief which these men accomplished entailed essentially the acceptance of mental derangement as illness rather than possession by devils.

The second revolution, according to Zilboorg and Henry, came some 300 years later through the work of Sigmund Freud, and paralleled a more general cultural development in art and politics, which demanded freedom of expression and a recognition of individual personality. Psychiatrically this revolution may be thought of as an emancipation of psychiatry from a purely physical and organic approach, based on the search for psychiatric 'disease' entities, an adequate nosology, and a preoccupation with possible physical, constitutional and hereditary causal factors. Freud directed attention to the possible *psychological* basis of mental illness, and initiated a treatment of a purely psychological kind. But, as we pointed out in the last chapter, he never entirely escaped from the organicist's frame of reference. Treatment was still to be on a one doctor–one patient basis, and the skilled manipulation of the 'transference' relationship in the consulting-room was thought to be the salient feature of the treatment process. The point is, perhaps, that mental illness was still regarded as very much an individual matter, or rather a matter of the individual in relation to the significant 'objects' (note the physical connotation) in his infantile environment.

The idea of establishing therapeutic communities as a method of treatment in their own right represents the third psychiatric revolution, which has gained momentum since the middle of this century. We are, perhaps, too close to our current climate of thought to discern objectively the drift in art and politics in relation to psychiatric developments, particularly in relation to the development of therapeutic communities. One might speculate about the failure of society to deal with mass unemployment in the thirties, the declining relevance of institutional religion, the rise of brutal totalitarian political régimes, the relapses into war and the cynicism engendered by the rising crime, drug addiction, mental illness and abortion rates in the Welfare State. Thus Halmos talks about the withdrawal from politics on the part of the psychological 'counsellor'—'vaccinated as he is now against political fever . . .'—to base his faith in man and society on mental health rather than political principles. And Erich Fromm (1955) advocates social reforms specifically designed to enhance mental health by creating a social order which is favourable to it. For Frank (1948), society itself *is* the patient, and treatment should be directed towards the group and not towards the individual. Foulkes and Anthony (1957) argue that psychiatrists should meet these demands of social philosophers by increasing the size of the 'therapeutic unit' from the individual to the group or to the community.

However that may be, more narrowly a number of factors have been distinguished which seem to have combined to promote this developing movement in psychiatry (Caine 1965). These may be summarized: (*a*) a growing dissatisfaction with individual psychotherapy, both with regard to the substantiated results and in terms of failure to cope with the sheer mass of the problem; (*b*) the emphasis of neo-Freudian writers such as Fromm (1943), Horney (1951) and Sullivan (1953) on interpersonal relations and cultural factors on neurotic breakdown; (*c*) the recognition of the deleterious effects on the inmates and staff of authoritarian, segregated, institutional régimes or 'total institutions' as Goffman (1958) describes them (Barton 1959, Martin 1955, 1962); (*d*) the application of social scientific theory to psychotherapy (Foulkes and Anthony 1957); (*e*) the increasing recognition of the importance of social experience in learning and communication processes in medicine, education and other fields (Anthony 1953, Cantril *et al.* 1949, Jaques 1951, Johnson 1953, Martin 1962, Revans 1964).

The therapeutic community treatment of neurosis, involving the psychotherapeutic exploitation of the interpersonal relations developing in the community along dynamic lines, is of recent origin, and owes its development to the synthesis of group methods of psychotherapy for the mentally ill and of transitional communities established for the resocialization of the chronic unemployed and ex-prisoners of war. In the medical field, one of the earliest attempts to extend the 'therapeutic unit' was made by British Army psychiatrists at the Northfield Army Neurosis Centre in Birmingham, where, according to Foulkes and Anthony, 'every aspect of the patient's life at the hospital was turned to therapeutic use. Everything that he did became treatment in the best sense of the word.' This lead was adopted in a number of specialized units after the war, and finally applied in a small number of mental hospitals in very recent years.

The use of transitional communities for assisting the passage of individuals within society from one social group to another is, according to Curle (1947), as old as society itself. The more specific use made of these communities to reduce an 'alienation' from society is perhaps of more recent origin. The state of alienation is frequently encountered amongst the inmate subculture of Goffman's 'total institutions'. Such physical separation of the inmates from the rest of the community may well involve the development of fundamentally different points of view, an increase in social distance between the two and an increase in the hostile stereotyping of each other. Many institutions such as prisons, tuberculosis sanatoria, homes for old people and mental and general hospitals may foster this process of 'institutionalization' in an extreme form. A children's home has been described by Bettelheim and Sylvester (1948) in which a rigid, comprehensive and impersonal régime allowed no scope for individual decisions by the inmate children and, demanding only compliance, led to apathy, lack of spontaneity and an incapacity for active adjustment to events which were commonplace to non-institutionalized children. The description of Goffman (1958) of these segregated, total institutions fits many hospitals for the chronic mentally ill. There is great social and psychological distance between staff and patients. Decisions about admission and discharge are made by the staff only, with patients often having little or no say in them. Contact with the outside world may be reduced to a minimum, and may be looked upon as a privilege. The patient may sleep, play and work in one place, and even the smallest detail, such as when he may wash or shave, may be decided for him. His clothes may not be his own, and they may well be shared with the other patients. Social experience may be reduced to a uniform, dehumanized level. The patient is no longer looked upon as a father, an employee, a friend, or a customer, but as a diagnosis, a chronic, my patient, or simply clinical material. In his study of the problem, Wing (1962) remarks that 'it is probably safe to say that most patients who have been continuously resident for more than two years in a mental hospital will have been exposed to many of the general features of total institutions'. In the specific institutionalization syndrome—to be distinguished from the schizophrenic syndrome—he included dependence on the institution, apathy about leaving, and lack of interest in outside activities.

Curle has given an anthropological description of the profound effects that such alienation and desocialization may have upon the individual. In his view, these effects involve the progressive disintegration of the individual's deep and extensive internalization of his culture, particularly with regard to social relations. Desocialization appears primarily as the individual's inability to use the stabilizing, internalized culture of his society, an inability which may promote 'quasi-psychotic' behaviour or, less severely, a loss of self-respect, guilt, feelings of inferiority and hostility. Therapeutic communities have been created to counteract these disintegrative processes.

A number of principles basic to therapeutic community treatment have been described by workers concerned with a variety of types of units and of inhabitants. Thus Curle writes that at the inception of the Civil Resettlement units for ex-prisoners of war a principle of fundamental importance was established largely through the influence of Army psychiatrists and psychologists, who, through pressure of numbers and time, had evolved group methods of treatment. This was an insistence on the use of democratic processes in the units, which had their ultimate sanction in the traditions of the British culture rather than in the Army under whose auspices the units were established. Again, one of the essential features of any method of psychological treatment is that of participation. But participation which arises from a spontaneous understanding of the related needs of the individual and the group cannot be imposed from without by an authoritarian régime. For this reason the Civil Resettlement Units were established on a purely *voluntary* basis. Curle considers that this voluntary principle was a basic condition, ensuring that the participants should feel that their needs and values were being respected, a prerequisite for the development of reciprocal interpersonal relations and for re-establishing within the individual the validity of the culture of his society. The ex-prisoner of war had developed profound feelings of insecurity and mistrust and a need for consistency in the basic values underlying roles and relationships. In this respect he has been described as a 'connoisseur in sincerity'. He accepted a role only in a community where acceptance of his values was genuine and consistent.

Thus decisions taken required a deep and wide acceptance of the principle of voluntary, democratic participation if the desired therapeutic aim was to be achieved. The translation of this principle into a sequence of decisions and consequent changes and collaborative action convinced the repatriate that his values had been clearly sanctioned both by the Army and by the home community, and that it was therefore safe to accept a role and take up relationships in civilian life.

In rather similar terms Rapoport (1960) has described the 'ideology' underlying the treatment procedures used at the Social Rehabilitation Unit (Jones 1952) when the unit was concerned with the long-term unemployed. He points out that this ideology, in common with most contemporary psychiatric innovations, is based on untested conviction. In general, the staff considered that their ideology served both the aims of treatment and the aims of rehabilitation—a view called into question by Rapoport, who defines psychological treatment as the alteration of the individual personality towards better intrapsychic integration, whereas rehabilitation involves the fitting of a particular personality to the demands of an existing social system. He suggests that some conflict between these orientations may often arise.

However, in the widest terms, the unit staff's conception of the fundamental character of a therapeutic community is based on three propositions, namely: (1) every activity, every relationship that develops in the unit is treatment; (2) all treatment is rehabilitation, involving both reorganization of personality and adjustment to the unit's social system and ultimately ordinary life outside the unit; (3) all patients should get the same treatment.

Subsuming these three basic beliefs, Rapoport abstracted four operative treatment processes around which staff discussion centred, namely, 'democratization', 'permissiveness', 'communalism', and 'reality confrontation'. His views on each may be summarized thus:

Democratization. This term refers to the view that all members of the community should share equally in therapeutic and administrative decisions. Conventional hospital status hierarchies should be replaced by a more equalitarian form of participation.

Democratization is seen as a way of getting patients to feel and take responsibility for others, of ventilating and treating problems to do with authority, and of improving communications between staff and patients.

Permissiveness. This refers to the belief that all members of the unit should tolerate from each other a wide range of distressing or 'deviant' behaviour. This tolerance would allow individuals to expose their behavioural difficulties and others to respond freely to them, so that both sides of the pattern of impersonal relations can be examined. The tension and anxiety generated by the display of symptoms and antisocial feelings can be used for therapeutic ends and for the understanding of the patients' psychopathology.

Communalism. By communalism is meant the emphasis on immediate, 'intimate' relationships engendered by the sharing of amenities, the informal use of first names, and the frank expression of thoughts and feelings. Such experiences are considered to counteract the social alienation resulting from discordant early family situations, and to promote the rehabilitative goals of 'participation' and social responsibility.

Reality-confrontation. This involves the continuous interpretation of their behaviour to the patients, as it is seen by most others, in order to counteract their maladaptive use of the defence mechanisms of denial, distortion and withdrawal, etc. The patient can only solve the problems he finds in his relations with others and with himself by facing them honestly.

Rapoport points out that values play a central role in the Social Rehabilitation Unit's conception of treatment. Indeed, he states that in a therapeutic community of this kind the assimilation of the unit's beliefs and value system is the essence of the therapy itself. He writes: 'In general, treatment goals call for a revision of distorted perceptions. The unit's method of achieving this implies patients' acceptance of unit values. When this occurs and is manifested in patients' behaviour, they are judged to have successfully "come into treatment".' The following six beliefs, he maintains, are held in common in all therapeutic communities:

'*a.* The total social organization in which the patient is involved—

and not only the relationship with the doctor—is seen as affecting the therapeutic outcome.

b. The social organization is not regarded as a routinized background to treatment, but as a vital force, useful for creating a milieu that will maximize therapeutic effects.

c. The core element in such an institutional context is the provision of opportunities for patients to take an active part in the affairs of the institution. . . .

d. *All* relationships within the hospital—those of patients among themselves as well as patients with staff—are regarded as potentially therapeutic. . . .

e. Aside from formal characteristics of structuring relationships, the *qualitative* atmosphere of the social environment is itself considered important therapeutically. This general orientation has reference to what is sometimes called the "emotional climate" of the institution. . . .

f. A high value is placed on communication *per se*. One basis for this value is an administrative one. It is considered valuable for people in one part of the organization to know what people in other parts are doing, thinking, and feeling. Furthermore, the act of communicating is thought to have an important morale and therapeutic effect for staff as well as patients. The content of communication is also considered valuable for treatment by making available, through a variety of channels, data supplementing the limited information that emerges in the doctor–patient relationship.'

With regard to the development of therapeutic communities in mental hospitals, however, the technique developed and the processes at work may well vary somewhat from one therapeutic community to another, depending upon the type of patients they serve and the assumptions of their staffs concerning the nature of their problems. Thus 'the therapeutic community' may be considered to be mainly a method of resocialization or rehabilitation, as in certain chronic wards concerned with the effects of institutionalization. In a neurosis unit the therapeutic community may be regarded as *the* primary form of 'medical' treatment, involving the uncovering and psychotherapy of unconscious, intrapsychic conflicts. In an acute admission unit in the same hospital it may be seen as a background against which physical treatments may most effectively be carried out. That there will be marked differences in the emphasis placed upon the value of certain procedures, relationships or communications in these different settings is obvious. To define these differences more precisely is the aim of the studies on attitudes to treatment reported in later chapters.

In writing of a neurosis unit in a mental hospital (personal communication) Martin considers that the fundamental aim of a therapeutic community is to provide an emotional climate in which the patient feels safe to express feelings previously repressed or inhibited as a result of real or imagined rejection by his parents in early childhood. Experience of life in the unit must convince the patient that what he feels to be bad and dangerous in his emotional life can find acceptance in the community, and that he will receive continuing help to understand it and come to terms with it. A therapeutic community, Martin says, must therefore be extremely accepting by conventional standards both of verbally expressed feelings and of actual behaviour. He thinks that limits must be placed on the extent of 'acting out', since extreme permissiveness under all circumstances can create terrifying feelings of insecurity when the patient is in the grip of very destructive fantasies. Patients need to feel that ultimately the staff are in control and that there are times when control may legitimately be exercised on therapeutic grounds, although no rules can be laid down about this varying balance between freedom and control. 'Judgment and intuition based upon intimate knowledge of the patients are the only guide.'

The maintenance of this permissive emotional climate is considered to be *the* most important function of the staff. The relationship between the staff and the patients is the primary means of maintaining the therapeutic process, and the attitudes of the staff have to be such that patients feel it is safe to be emotionally sincere and honest in all relationships within the unit. This means that the staff, too, must be sincere about their feelings, and Martin sees this as the most difficult and yet crucial therapeutic problem. What is necessary is a break from the conventional staff relationships, etiquette and roles emphasized in the traditional training of medical staff and nurses, which is only possible if the staff have the goodwill and readiness to tolerate the psychological stresses involved and the opportunity to work together for long periods of time.

For Martin, a therapeutic relationship in a therapeutic community implies involvement with the patient, and an attitude of encouragement of a relatively detached inquiry by the patient into his own and other patients' problems. The development and opening up of the transference at an early stage in treatment is the basis of the psychotherapy in the groups and ward meetings, to be achieved by focusing the attention of patients upon their emotional responses to each other and to the staff in the 'here and now' situation. Patients should be expected to take as much responsibility for themselves and the running of the unit as possible, with a minimum of intervention from the staff. He emphasizes that psychiatry, more than any other branch of medicine, gives expression to the philosophy of life and the values of its practitioners. In his own view, for example, the development of 'consciousness' is more valuable and fundamental than the relief of suffering alone—a view which has been foreshadowed in a number of systems of religious thought.

In articles by the Claybury Hospital staff (Shoenberg, in press) certain recurrent themes supporting Rapoport's observations can be distinguished, namely an emphasis on 'communication', 'the expression and understanding of true feeling', 'the patient's illness is part of a sick family', 'warmth and concern', 'acceptance and respect for the individual', 'willingness to work with people rather than to direct them', 'relaxation of the traditional hierarchical system', 'roles in the staff team are not sharply defined', 'everything that happens to the patients is part of treatment', 'the total atmosphere of the hospital is valuable as treatment, "permissiveness" '. Thus Pippard (1966), with regard to an acute admission unit using a wide range of physical treatments, writes that the *setting* in which treatment takes place is of great importance 'for good or ill', and quotes the World Health Organisation Expert Committee on Mental Health (1953): 'The atmosphere of the mental hospital is the most important single factor in the efficacy of the treatment given.' Implicit in this, he writes, is the idea that the whole of a patient's life in hospital is to be seen as treatment, and not just the time spent with his doctor or receiving some kind of physical attention. 'When we talk of a "good" hospital we refer, I believe, not *only* to the quality of the medical attention, or the research achievements of its staff, but also to the kind of relationships which exist between the staff and between the hospital and the community it serves.' Very similar points have been made by Crocket (1961) with regard to his treatment orientation at the Ingrebourne Centre. He emphasizes the distinction made by Rapoport between treatment and rehabilitation, and considers that in the therapeutic community both staff and patients alike develop a relationship 'which is with the community as a whole'. This relationship is like the therapeutic relationships of individual therapy, and must be preserved even at the expense of individual treatment relationships which might possibly develop in the community.

There is little doubt that amongst therapeutic community organizers and participants there is a considerable area of agreement on the basic theoretical principles involved, and this without any great interchange of personnel, regular exchange of information or research. What is equally true is that there is a considerable degree of ambivalence amongst staff and patients on the extent that these principles can in fact be put into practice. Although scientific evidence is lacking, one suspects that the therapeutic effectiveness of the various types of therapeutic communities varies considerably, not only from time to time in their own life histories but also compared with each other. If therapeutic effectiveness depends upon how much therapeutic community ideology is in fact put into practice, this will depend upon the individual staff members and patients involved at any one time. Individuals vary considerably in their capacity to tolerate relatively unstructured treatment situations, to relinquish the safety of formal role relationships, control and authority, and to communicate freely on an informal, personal basis.

It is a debatable point whether it is possible fully to develop a therapeutic treatment régime within an already existing larger treatment organization, such as a mental hospital staffed by traditionally trained doctors, nurses and administrators. The stresses and strains involved in such an attempt have been described by Martin (1962, p. 57), who considers in writing of staff problems that 'A genuine inner change of attitude is needed, and such a process takes a long time in all of us and often involves considerable upset and personal suffering.' For those of us who have been associated with an attempt to transform a whole, large, traditional mental hospital this does not appear to be an overstatement. In a hospital where the selection of staff is considerably limited and where medical and administrative responsibilities are 'laid down', opposition to the basic principles of therapeutic community treatment is to be expected at all levels. It is not clear, for example, just how much staff and patients in a large organization *can* be involved in decisions in the directly democratic way possible in the smaller specialized and independent therapeutic communities of the Civil Resettlement Units and the Henderson Hospital. It is not possible to *impose* therapeutic community ideology on others who may well be incapable of working in this way, or, indeed, on patients who may find this treatment incompatible. In any event, such an imposition would run counter to the idealized democratic process.

The situation is further complicated by the fact that consultants within a hospital have the right to decide their own methods of treatment in the absence of unequivocal scientific evidence for the superiority of one treatment over another. This fact is clearly understood by both staff and patients, and applies equally well to therapeutic communities. One suspects with regard to the latter that the personality of the medical director is of prime importance for effective treatment, democratic principles notwithstanding. The degree to which he will be able to delegate responsibility and to abdicate in favour of group decisions will obviously be a personal matter, and yet a vital one. For example, as one senior nurse in a therapeutic community has remarked, members must feel that what they have to say in the various meetings will have a *real* bearing on subsequent action. As soon as the staff begin to feel that they are being encouraged to talk simply for some supposed psychotherapeutic end for themselves, they will become, as he put it, doubly frustrated. At the same time, as in other social movements, the 'leader' must be something of a charismatic figure if the movement is to sustain its momentum. For a therapeutic community to become static may be fatal. Presumably the momentum must be in the directions of democratization, permissiveness, communalism and reality-confrontation. The fate of the therapeutic community neurosis unit at Claybury Hospital, closed in the absence of the leader on sick leave, is an object lesson in the problems of staff and patient dependency and the fears that can be aroused on all sides when the official leader is absent.

The opportunities presented for basic research in social processes by the advent of these units are unique. Until this work is done, there would seem to be no chance of resolving the inevitable and endless conflicts which arise with the establishment of these communities within existing authoritarian, traditional social institutions.

CHAPTER 4

A questionnaire measure of attitudes to treatment

From the last three chapters it emerges that a person who finds himself a patient in a mental hospital can expect to receive treatment less on the basis of scientific research and discovery than on the assumptions and beliefs of those responsible for his care. Nobody would be in a position to give him an accurate description of the 'cause' of his condition, nor could they with any certainty estimate the possibility of a 'cure'. Nevertheless, his treatment will probably be carried out against a background of medical omniscience, which may well lead him to believe, whether he is given drugs, psychotherapy or leucotomy, that those involved in his treatment know what they are doing. The need for research and evaluation is enormous, even though a significant proportion of practitioners in the field probably feel that their own experience is sufficient justification for their assumptions.

Yet the problems of research are depressingly complex. In evaluating the effectiveness of a method of treatment, it is not just a matter of comparing a 'group' of patients treated by 'psychotherapy' with a 'group' treated by some other method or not treated at all. The factors which contribute to successful treatment may reside in both patients and therapists, and may interact between the two in unexpected ways. Such factors, moreover, need not necessarily be those which the particular theory holds to be important, but may lie in phenomena of which the theory takes no account. In general, most research workers (see, for example, reviews by Bergin 1966 and Kiesler 1966) have moved beyond the crudely naïve approach of Eysenck in his much publicized denial of the usefulness of psychotherapy (1952, 1960). For example, in his demonstration that psychotherapy did no better than no treatment at all, Eysenck took no account of the fact, well documented by Bergin (1966), that some therapists do better than chance with their patients, and some do worse; thus, although the overall results of psychotherapy appeared to be no better than no therapy at all, Eysenck did not consider variability in therapists' performance. One therefore needs a very much finer analysis of the variables involved before jumping to sweeping conclusions about the usefulness of any method of treatment.

A first and essential step in attempting the scientific evaluation of any method of treatment is to arrive at a satisfactory definition of that method; and it is with our own attempts to do this in the context of the therapeutic community that we shall be concerned in this chapter.

Our feeling at the beginning of this research was that the way in which the therapeutic community treatment at Claybury Hospital is put into practice must depend less on the general theory—as outlined, for example, by D. V. Martin in his book (1962)—than on the more specific views of the doctors and nurses who put it into practice and of the patients who experience it. For this reason we felt we needed a measure of the attitudes to treatment and the views concerning their role in the community of those involved. A questionnaire seemed to be the simplest and most direct answer to this problem.

CONSTRUCTION OF THE QUESTIONNAIRE

In order to avoid as far as possible building into the questionnaire our own assumptions about what people feel to be important in treatment, we decided that we should conduct 'non-directive' tape-recorded interviews with a small sample of doctors, nurses, patients, and other staff concerned in the care of the mentally ill. Ideally we should have liked to interview staff who subscribed to more traditional treatment methods than those used in the Claybury therapeutic community, but considerations of time and facility limited us to the Claybury population. However, this bias was to some extent mitigated, in that most of the staff we interviewed had spent a considerable proportion of their career in other institutions and were able to draw useful comparisons between different types of treatment; and again, not all of those we talked to were enthusiastic supporters of the therapeutic community approach.

We had no fixed idea about how many interviews should be conducted, and in practice stopped interviewing when we felt that the material was becoming repetitive. The form of the interviews was, as already mentioned, as far as possible non-directive: respondents talked about how they felt about the treatment, what they felt the problems, advantages and disadvantages were, their relationships within the ward and the hospital hierarchy, and so on.

In all, thirty-nine interviews were carried out: five with doctors, eight with nurses, two with psychiatric social workers, one with an occupational therapist, and twenty-three with patients, both neurotic and psychotic.

We then listened to the recordings, noting points which tended to be raised more than once and which appeared significant for our inquiry. These were put into the questionnaire in the form of statements which could be rated from 'strongly agree' through 'agree', 'uncertain', 'disagree' to 'strongly disagree'. These statements conformed as nearly as possible to the respondents' original formulations during interview, though we reversed some statements from positive to negative in order to achieve a reasonable balance between different types and directions of answer, and clothed some statements which were specific to Claybury problems in a more general form.

The original questionnaire contained 126 items scored from five ('strongly agree') to one ('strongly disagree'). After a preliminary examination of the results obtained with this instrument, and a relatively superficial analysis of the differences between the answers of therapeutic community doctors as compared with medical staff of other orientations (see Caine and Smail 1966), we eliminated questions which yielded an excessively skewed distribution of scores (i.e. with which nearly all respondents either agreed or disagreed), as well as those which were framed so ambiguously as to be of doubtful value. This left us with a questionnaire of seventy-five items, the final version of which is reproduced below.

The questionnaire

This questionnaire is in the form of statements with which you may agree or disagree more or less strongly. We should be grateful if you would indicate your answer by putting a circle round the appropriate letters, which are explained as follows:

SA	means	*Strongly agree*
A	means	*Agree or tend to agree*
U	means	*Uncertain whether you agree or disagree*
D	means	*Disagree or tend to disagree*
SD	means	*Strongly disagree*

[These letters in fact appeared next to each item of the questionnaire.]

Please answer *all* the questions.

A. Set out below are some activities which may be part of a *nurse's* job. Please indicate *how much you would agree or disagree with a nurse working in this way* by circling the letters next to each item in the way described above.

1. Keeping discipline on the ward.
2. Making sure that patients don't have time to think about their problems.
3. Suggesting to patients the underlying reasons for what they (the patients) say or do.
4. Advising patients on how to cope with their difficulties.
5. Working alongside patients when they are working on the ward.
6. Taking a great interest in theoretical matters, such as reading books on psychiatry in spare time.
7. Taking care not to show too much interest in patients' deeper problems in order to avoid getting involved.
8. Taking care to conceal own personality from the patients.
9. Looking out for trouble-makers on the ward, and making sure they don't get away with anything.
10. Talking to the patients and trying to get to the root of their problems.

B. On the following pages are various statements about the types of treatment, the patients and the staff in a hospital such as this. Please indicate as before *how far you agree or disagree with the statements.*

11. It is important to have the ward organized according to strict rules.
12. Patients have to get worse before they get better.
13. It's more important for patients to talk about their relationships within the ward than to talk about their relationships outside.
14. Physical treatments are a means of getting through to the patients, but not a cure in themselves.
15. Doctors should be more honest with the patients and not hide so much behind a 'mask'.
16. Patients should be discouraged from developing feelings towards staff members.
17. It is an important part of treatment for patients to believe that the doctors are all-powerful.
18. It's important to give patients direct encouragement to put knowledge about themselves gained in the ward setting into action at home.
19. One of the most important things in treatment is to establish the correct diagnosis.
20. Staff being too friendly towards patients makes for poor discipline on the ward.
21. Staff are there to guide the treatment rather than help the patients directly.
22. Once the senior doctor has made up his mind, nobody should question his decision.
23. The nurse's uniform is bad because it makes a barrier between nurses and patients.
24. Nurses should never disagree with doctors in front of the patients.
25. Nurses have to spend too much time attending to administrative matters rather than to the patients.
26. The atmosphere on the ward depends on the doctor in charge.

27. The good psychiatric nurse is entirely free from psychological difficulties.
28. Nurses should always consult the doctors about the best way to handle a patient.
29. The doctor's knowledge makes them the only people capable of treating the patients.
30. Doctors can nearly always interpret the meaning of what patients do and say better than nurses.
31. Doctors must not be afraid to make mistakes which will lay them open to criticism and attack from patients.
32. There is fundamentally no difference between staff and patients.
33. The doctor's choice of treatment for a patient is more a matter of his personal opinion than of proved fact.
34. The nurse should always make sure that the patients are neat and well-groomed.
35. How effective a person is in treating a patient depends more on his or her personality than on the particular job or amount of knowledge he or she may have.
36. Doctors should not mix with the patients too much.
37. More than anything else, the doctor's job is to guide what other people do, rather than do things himself.
38. A patient should not be expected to discuss really personal problems with the other patients.
39. The point of a patient being in hospital is to have his mind taken off his problems.
40. The doctor's analysis of the patient's feelings towards him is the most important thing in treatment.
41. It is important for the patient to be himself on the ward, even if it means being unpleasant.
42. The patient is helped most by people he can see as individuals rather than as professional workers.
43. One of the most helpful things in treatment is for a patient to realize that he is not the only one with problems.
44. Doctors know things about the patients' personal problems which the other patients do not know.
45. It helps patients to realize that staff can have psychological difficulties themselves.

46. The aim of treatment should be to rid patients of psychiatric symptoms, not to change them as people.
47. Patients would be helped more if they could see their doctors individually more often.
48. Patients should not call nurses by their Christian names.
49. Patients often don't know much about the treatment they are getting.
50. A patient will not get better if he does not talk about his difficulties.
51. Treatment in psychiatry is a scientific technique and should not involve the doctor's feelings.
52. Doctors do not know as much about the patients as the nurses.
53. It is important that the doctor should not show his real feelings to the patients.
54. The patient does not really get better until he actually tries out new ways of feeling and behaving.
55. It would be helpful to the patients if the doctors attended ward socials and similar functions more often.
56. Once the patients start to see other people's problems, they start to see their own.
57. Patients' relationships with people on the ward are often similar to their relationships at home.
58. A patient will only really be helped by someone who is personally concerned about him.
59. Practical experience and life on the ward are more important in the patient's treatment than being given theoretical knowledge about himself.
60. Comments made to a patient about himself can make him face his problems even when they are not accurate.
61. One of the most important things in treatment is for patients to learn how other people feel.
62. Treatment does not get rid of the patient's problems, but enables him to feel better about them.
63. Nurse–patient relationships can be just as effective in treatment as doctor–patient relationships.
64. Practical experience is more important than theoretical knowledge for doctors.

65. There is not much difference between a good doctor and a good nurse except that the doctor is the one who prescribes the drugs.
66. Doctors tend to look at patients as interesting cases rather than as individual people.
67. Patients usually feel inferior to the doctors.
68. Patients often get better mainly through contact with one or two people.
69. Feeling that the doctors have the sole power to decide about their admission and discharge makes it impossible for some patients to confide in them completely.
70. There should be more therapeutic group meetings in the ward.
71. Physical treatments (tablets, electrical treatment, etc.) are on the whole more effective than any other kind of treatment.
72. There is usually a 'crisis' point in treatment after which patients start to get better.
73. The doctor's knowledge and experience means that he is the only person capable of keeping treatment on the right track.
74. A ward in a mental hospital should be kept up to the same standards of cleanliness and efficiency by the staff as a ward in a general hospital.
75. Staff often fail to give sufficient reassurance and support to patients who are worried by the treatment.

Clearly, it seemed likely that a number of these items would tend to group together to form scales (or 'components') representing certain basic attitudes. In order to identify these attitudes, the questionnaire scores were analysed by computer (by the method of 'principal components'). This analysis was carried out independently for samples of psychiatrists, nurses and patients.

ATTITUDES OF PSYCHIATRISTS

A request to complete the questionnaire was made to the medical staff of sixteen mental hospitals which were scattered over a wide area of Britain. Respondents were asked to complete the questionnaire from the point of view of treatment in acute admission wards or neurosis units. No response was forthcoming from two hospitals, while the response from other hospitals varied from 10 per cent to 100 per cent. Although there are obvious methodological shortcomings in the rather loose nature of this method of sampling, practical considerations of time and distance made a more sophisticated approach impossible. In all, seventy-nine doctors were included in the principal components analysis of scores on the questionnaire items. Of these, twenty-eight were consultant psychiatrists, twenty-three were senior psychiatrists below the rank of consultant, and twenty-six were junior psychiatrists or doctors in training. We were unable to identify the status of two respondents.

Results

In considering the statistical analysis, we decided to limit our interest to the first three components extracted, since these seemed both psychologically the most meaningful as well as being the most important from the technical point of view (accounting for more of the variance). Table 1 shows the questionnaire items which go to make up these three components for the psychiatrist sample. For the technically interested, we should say that these are the items having a saturation of at least $\pm 0{\cdot}15$ on each normalized component; also shown are the latent roots and percentages of variance accounted for by the components.

An inspection of these three components suggests that each is associated with a number of attitudes which might be considered psychologically distinct. It should, of course, be borne in mind that scores at the negative pole of a component imply the opposite of the views expressed rather than minimal acceptance of them.

Component 1 appears to be associated with an emphasis on physical treatments, and with the view that personality and personal relationships are relatively insignificant in treatment. The accent is more on formal role-relationships and 'traditional' hospital discipline, with collusion amongst the staff to maintain a united front before the patients in the event of staff disagreement. Demonstration of emotional or personality characteristics on the part of the staff to the patients is taboo. The doctor's authority should be absolute and unquestioned.

Component 2 strongly emphasizes the importance of interpersonal relations in the ward setting, group dynamics, the disturbing nature of treatment, and the central role played by the doctor as leader and interpreter to be seen as an all-powerful and to some degree mysterious figure by the patients.

TABLE I. QUESTIONNAIRE ITEMS WITH A SATURATION OF AT LEAST ±0·15 ON EACH COMPONENT FOR THE PSYCHIATRIST SAMPLE

	Questionnaire items		
	Component 1	*Component 2*	*Component 3*
	2 (+)	12 (+)	4 (−)
	14 (−)	13 (+)	6 (−)
	16 (+)	14 (+)	15 (−)
	23 (−)	15 (−)	17 (+)
	24 (+)	17 (+)	18 (−)
	29 (+)	21 (+)	25 (−)
	34 (+)	25 (−)	34 (−)
	35 (−)	28 (+)	40 (+)
	41 (−)	29 (+)	49 (−)
	46 (+)	30 (+)	52 (−)
	48 (+)	37 (+)	56 (−)
	51 (+)	40 (+)	64 (−)
	54 (−)	56 (+)	68 (−)
	63 (−)	60 (+)	69 (−)
	65 (−)	61 (+)	71 (−)
	71 (+)	62 (+)	
	74 (+)	72 (+)	
Latent root	12·32	4·92	4·24
Per cent variance	16·43	6·56	5·65

Component 3, although rather more difficult to interpret, seems to lay more importance on the individual relationship and analysis of transference between patient and doctor than on physical treatments or relationships between patients or between patients and nurses. Here again it appears to be an advantage for the patient to view the doctor as omnipotent and inscrutable. An opposition to dispensing direct advice to patients and an emphasis on theoretical training suggest a preference for interpretative psychotherapy.

Thus the underlying theme here appears to be primarily one of treatment orientations, with the components emphasizing (at the positive pole): (1) physical treatments, (2) group therapy, (3) individual psychotherapy.

Validation of the components

In order to substantiate this hypothesis concerning treatment orientations, doctors were assigned to five groups, namely physical treatments (P), group therapy (G), individual psychotherapy (I), therapeutic community treatment (C), and eclectic (E). Respondents were allocated to the appropriate groups according to their known treatment practice, or, where this was not known, according to their response to a check-list. In the latter case, though asked to tick only one orientation, eight respondents felt it necessary to specify two; and in this eventuality the most reasonable course, and the one which put least strain on the data, seemed to be to allocate these subjects to both groups. Eight doctors were unable to classify themselves within this framework, and were dropped from subsequent group comparisons.

We hypothesized that, if our interpretation of the components was correct, doctors oriented primarily towards physical treatments should score highest on component 1, group therapists on component 2, and individual psychotherapists highest on component 3. Table 2 sets out the mean scores on the three components of the various groups in descending order of magnitude. Significant differences between the criterion group (e.g. physical treatment oriented doctors in the case of component 1) and the other groups are asterisked. Tests of statistical significance were Mann–Whitney *U* tests or *t* tests as appropriate. Numbers in groups vary between components, since, in the cases where some respondents were assigned to two groups, they were retained only in the criterion group for each component.

TABLE 2. MEAN SCORES ON COMPONENTS 1, 2 AND 3 OF PSYCHIATRISTS GROUPED ACCORDING TO TREATMENT ORIENTATION

	Group				
	P (N=16)	E (N=26)	I (N=7)	G (N=8)	C (N=19)
Component 1	+2·48	+1·15	−0·58*	−1·16†	−3·46‡
	G (N=10)	C (N=14)	E (N=26)	I (N=5)	P (N=14)
Component 2	+1·24	+0·20	−0·04	−0·18	−0·47
	I (N=8)	G (N=7)	C (N=18)	E (N=26)	P (N=15)
Component 3	+1·31	+0·33	−0·15*	−0·55†	−0·60*

* different from criterion group $p < 0{\cdot}05$
† different from criterion group $p < 0{\cdot}01$
‡ different from criterion group $p < 0{\cdot}001$

P = Physical treatments
G = Group therapy
I = Individual psychotherapy
C = Community therapy
E = Eclectic

An examination of table 2 bears out the predictions made about the nature of the three components, although with varying degrees of differentiation. In addition, the rank order of the group means is much in accordance with what one would expect from a knowledge of the types of treatment involved. Of the two non-criterion groups (i.e. community therapists and eclectics), the latter tend to fall centrally in the table, whereas the community therapists are characterized by an extreme negative position on component 1 (being significantly different from all other groups in this respect, p varying from $<0{\cdot}001$ to $<0{\cdot}02$, when groups I and G are combined). Indeed, in comparing physical treatment doctors and community therapy doctors on this component, there is an overlap of only two individuals between the two groups (the total number involved being thirty-five).

From this it seems clear that the questions concerning treatment over which psychiatrists differ are not simply matters of scientific dispute about the suitability of specific remedies for specific illnesses, but include more complex constellations of attitudes which colour their approach to the patients and to other staff in the ward setting in a very much more general way. The criterion groups in the present analysis have little in common beyond an apparent belief in the very central place of the doctor in treatment from the point of view both of knowledge and of authority. Even this feature, which to many may seem little more than the honest recognition of an obvious truth, seems, both from the preliminary analysis of the questionnaire (see Caine and Smail 1966) and from the findings reported above, to be disputed by some psychiatrists at least (e.g. those who are oriented towards therapeutic community treatment). The mode of relationship between doctor and patient (and doctor and staff) is a bone of contention at the root of many a dispute and a good deal of resentment between members of the profession (see, for example, Chertok 1966)—a fact with which all but the most fortunate workers in mental hospitals will be familiar.

The need of some psychiatrists to maintain 'psychological distance' from their patients, which is to some extent evident in our present data, has been challenged by several writers within recent years (for example, Jourard 1964; see chapter 2 of this book); and one might speculate that theoretical rationalizations for avoidance on the therapist's part of exposure of himself to the patients as a fallible human being with a personality of his own may be based on the fantasy that the slightest unbending would lead to the unleashing of a chaotic set of circumstances over which he would have no control. This is to some extent similar to the situation in which the anxiety neurotic often finds himself: he or she must stay within the security of the home for fear of what might happen, or what he or she might do, if allowed to roam abroad. The 'psychologically distant' doctor would seem to be setting a strange example to patients whose openness to himself he is often importunately, if tacitly, demanding. Presumably the efficacy or inefficacy of such an approach must depend on the importance of setting, or being, an example.

It is apparent from our data that differences in orientation cannot simply be ascribed to differences in types of patients treated; and the fact that the majority of respondents in the present sample are of senior status suggests that the views expressed may be put to practical application and are held with some conviction. While it is true that the marked difference of opinion between members of a single profession which our data reflect must rest to a large extent on training and experience, the absence of anything approaching conclusive evidence in favour of one approach or another suggests that personality may play an equally important role. This is a point upon which some light will be thrown later in this book.

The present findings again accentuate the difficulties inherent in studies comparing different methods of treatment. Treatment cannot simply be viewed as a mechanical process independent of the men and women who carry it out, and the attitudes related to a specific orientation must be defined and assessed if one is to arrive at a reasonable idea of the variables involved. Again, it would be virtually impossible for one individual to employ several different methods of treatment in a comparative study (as has often enough been attempted)—whatever his 'scientific objectivity', it is doubtful whether he would be able sincerely to reproduce the attitudes correlated with a number of different orientations. These observations would tend to reinforce doubts expressed earlier in this chapter about the validity of the Eysenckian kind of argument against the value of psychotherapy.

ATTITUDES OF NURSES

The nursing sample was drawn from ten hospitals, again representing a geographically wide area. Only questionnaires from nurses working in acute admission or neurosis units were included in the analysis. Here again it was from a practical point of view impossible to employ a strictly controlled sampling technique, since response to the questionnaire was entirely voluntary, with no pressure being brought to bear on potential respondents. Strict confidentiality was ensured. Liaison between ourselves and the nursing population was in most cases mediated by the medical staff of the hospitals concerned. Completed questionnaires were seen only by ourselves. The responses of a total of 120 nurses were included in the computer analysis. Table 3 shows the composition of the sample in terms of sex and professional grade.

TABLE 3. COMPOSITION OF SAMPLE OF NURSES

Professional grade	*Male*	*Female*
Chief male nurse/Matron	–	1
Assistant CMN/Assistant matron	5	4
Charge nurse/Sister	20	21
Staff nurse	20	11
Student nurse	17	17
Nursing assistant	–	2
Total	62	56

(No information regarding sex or status in two cases)

As with the psychiatrist sample, we shall consider here the first three components to be extracted by the principal components analysis. Table 4 shows the questionnaire items having a saturation of at least $\pm 0{\cdot}15$ on the normalized components, as well as the latent root and percentage of variance accounted for by each component.

Component 1 appears to have much in common with its counterpart for the psychiatrist sample—in fact about 50 per cent of the items are identical. In this case, as with the psychiatrists, component 1 seems to reflect an emphasis on formal discipline, hygiene, an impersonal approach towards patients, and a particular emphasis on the physical aspects of nursing and treatment. Also explicit in this component is an acceptance of the absolute authority and power of the doctor. It would seem that the positive pole of this component conforms closely to the stereotype of the attitudes of the traditional general hospital nurse.

Components 2 and 3 in the present sample do not appear to be as closely related as component 1 to the corresponding components

TABLE 4. QUESTIONNAIRE ITEMS WITH A SATURATION OF AT LEAST ±0·15 ON EACH COMPONENT FOR THE SAMPLE OF NURSES

	Questionnaire items		
	Component 1	*Component 2*	*Component 3*
	1 (+)	5 (−)	12 (−)
	2 (+)	10 (−)	13 (−)
	7 (+)	15 (−)	20 (−)
	11 (+)	35 (−)	25 (+)
	16 (+)	36 (+)	32 (+)
	17 (+)	41 (−)	33 (+)
	19 (+)	42 (−)	47 (+)
	20 (+)	43 (−)	49 (+)
	22 (+)	45 (−)	55 (+)
	24 (+)	54 (−)	60 (−)
	29 (+)	55 (−)	62 (+)
	34 (+)	56 (−)	66 (+)
	39 (+)	59 (−)	69 (+)
	47 (+)	61 (−)	70 (+)
	48 (+)	64 (−)	72 (−)
	51 (+)	65 (−)	75 (+)
	53 (+)		
	71 (+)		
	74 (+)		
Latent root	10·42	6·03	3·99
Per cent variance	13·89	8·04	5·32

n the psychiatrist sample. Component 2 in this case emphasizes primarily, at the positive pole, the necessity for maintaining a detached relationship with patients and presenting them with a professional *persona* aimed at avoiding any kind of personal or emotional relationship with them. It is also thought to be important that doctors should maintain a considerable measure of 'psychological distance' from patients. The negative pole here stresses the importance of psychological proximity between staff and patients (and amongst patients themselves), in which the member of staff, whether nurse or doctor, is willing to expose his own personality to the patients.

Component 3 is very much more difficult to interpret, but it appears if anything to reflect a protective attitude towards patients and an identification with them, together with a critical attitude towards authority, particularly as this is represented by the medical staff.

Comparison of nursing attitudes between hospitals

Six hospitals well known for their approach to treatment were selected for comparison with regard to the attitudes of nursing staff. Of these six, two were mental hospitals using largely conventional methods of treatment, two were mental hospitals specializing in therapeutic community methods of treatment, and two were specialized units for the treatment of non-psychotic patients. Table 5 shows the means and standard deviations of scores on the three components of nursing staff from these hospitals. Hospitals A and B represent the therapeutic community hospitals, C and D the conventional treatment hospitals, and E and F the specialized units.

TABLE 5. MEAN SCORES OF HOSPITALS ON THREE COMPONENTS

		Component 1		Component 2		Component 3	
Hospital	*N*	*Mean*	*S.D.*	*Mean*	*S.D.*	*Mean*	*S.D.*
A	15	−1·67	1·82	−1·60	1·71	−0·72	1·39
B	23	−1·48	2·35	−0·22	2·50	0·35	1·99
C	8	2·48	1·33	1·01	2·59	1·32	2·44
D	23	3·07	2·58	0·22	2·29	0·24	1·28
E	10	−3·52	1·41	−0·86	1·94	−1·78	1·33
F	7	−3·34	2·52	2·44	1·13	−1·59	1·08

In view of the different types of patients involved, the four mental hospitals and the two specialized units were considered separately in the first instance for the sake of testing for significant differences between mean scores.

On component 1, an overall difference was found between the

four mental hospitals (analysis of variance F ratio = 21·72, $p < 0·001$). Further (t test) comparisons between the individual hospitals showed that this result resides in the difference between the two conventional treatment hospitals (C and D) on the one hand and the two therapeutic community hospitals (A and B) on the other ($t = 8·00, p < 0·001$). With regard to the two specialized units (E and F), no significant difference between the means emerged. Thus a further comparison was made between these two combined and hospitals A and B on the one hand and hospitals C and D on the other. The result of this comparison is that hospitals E and F are significantly different from hospitals A and B ($t = 2·93$, $p < 0·01$) and from hospitals C and D ($t = 9·35$, $p < 0·001$). These differences are summarized in table 6.

On component 2, analysis of variance between the four mental hospitals proved insignificant ($F = 2·70$). A comparison between the means of hospitals E and F was, however, significant ($t = 3·83$, $p < 0·002$). Comparison between hospital E and the combined

TABLE 6. SIGNIFICANT DIFFERENCES BETWEEN HOSPITALS ON COMPONENT I

Hospitals	*N*	*Mean*	*S.D.*	*t*	*p <*
A+B	38	−1·56	2·16		
v.					
C+D	31	2·92	2·34	8·00	0·001
A+B	38	−1·56	2·16		
v.					
E+F	17	−3·44	1·96	2·94	0·01
C+D	31	2·92	2·34		
v.					
E+F	17	−3·44	1·96	9·35	0·001

hospitals A+B+C+D was not significant. Hospital F, on the other hand, was significantly different from the combined mental hospitals ($t = 2·90$, $p < 0·01$). These differences are summarized in table 7 (p. 76).

On component 3, neither an analysis of variance between, hospitals A, B, C and D, nor a t test comparison between hospitals

TABLE 7. SIGNIFICANT DIFFERENCES BETWEEN HOSPITALS ON COMPONENT 2

Hospitals	*N*	*Mean*	*S.D.*	*t*	*p* <
A+B+C+D	69	−0·23	2·43		
v.					
F	7	2·44	1·13	2·90	0·01
E	10	−0·86	1·94		
v.					
F	7	2·44	1·13	3·83	0·002

E and F proved significant. However, the combined mean of hospitals E and F was significantly different from the combined mean of hospitals A, B, C and D ($t = 4{\cdot}04$, $p < 0{\cdot}001$). This comparison is shown in table 8.

TABLE 8. SIGNIFICANT DIFFERENCE BETWEEN HOSPITALS ON COMPONENT 3

Hospitals	*N*	*Mean*	*S.D.*	*t*	*p* <
A+B+C+D	69	0·19	1·84		
v.					
E+F	17	−1·71	1·22	4·04	0·001

Table 6 shows that the mean scores of the hospitals on component 1 are in the following order: C+D, A+B, E+F. That hospitals E and F are lowest on this component is not surprising in view of the fact that they do not admit psychotic patients, and consequently have less need for physical treatments. Although hospitals A, B, C and D are similar in that they admit all types of mental patients, nursing attitudes differ considerably, with the therapeutic community hospital staff approaching those of the specialized units. The fact that the hospitals are distributed in this way supports the interpretation of component 1 already advanced. Thus, although the therapeutic community mental hospitals (A and B) use physical treatments, presumably they do so with less enthusiasm and in a less disciplinarian and formal setting.

Table 7 picks out hospital F as differing from all the others. It is surprising that the analysis of variance did not yield a significant difference between the means of the four mental hospitals, since one would have predicted that the therapeutic community hospitals would have been significantly lower on this component. Most authorities on therapeutic communities stress the necessity in treatment for the reduction of the kind of 'psychological distance' maintained by staff in more traditional settings between themselves and the patients, indeed between all members of the community. Although the means of the hospitals are in the expected direction on this component, this aspect of therapeutic community treatment does not appear to have gained complete acceptance among the nursing staff. Hospital F is well known for its emphasis on more traditional psychoanalytic techniques. Since the Freudian view of the therapeutic relationship stresses the importance of objectivity and avoidance of involvement on the part of the therapist, it is scarcely surprising that the nursing staff of hospital F score highly on this component.

Table 8 is hard to interpret without tendentiousness. However, one might hypothesize that in view of the fact that hospitals E and F are very much smaller than the others, with a more rigorously selected staff and a more highly specialized treatment programme, the nursing staff may well be more highly identified with the aims of the treatment and the methods of the medical staff.

In general, although the technical shortcomings of the research technique in this study are obvious, certain sharp, meaningful differences in attitude to the theory and practice of mental nursing have been demonstrated. The fact that nursing attitudes differ so markedly from hospital to hospital makes it meaningless to talk of 'a training' for mental nurses or 'a treatment' for mental patients. Although it would be a commonplace observation to the professional in the field, that such a diversity exists may come as a surprise to the general public, who may well have been misled by apparently authoritative pronouncements made in the press or on television by leading psychiatrists into believing that the type of treatment and care open to them will be regulated only by the march of science. It will depend much more upon the 'catchment area' in which they live.

An earlier study by one of us (Caine 1964) compared the interest patterns of general hospital nurses with those of nurses working in the therapeutic community, scores being derived from the Kuder Preference Record Personal Form A. In view of their similarity to some of the findings mentioned above, it may be of interest to summarize here the findings of that study: 'The differences between the two groups lie in scales C (preference for working with ideas) and E (preference for directing others); here the therapeutic community nurses show a marked preference for dealing with ideas and behaviour in the abstract as opposed to an active, "adventurous", social and business life. This, together with their very marked absence of authoritarian attitudes as measured by scale E, is of direct relevance to their work as mental nurses in a therapeutic community. . . . The differences in interest between the general nurses and the therapeutic community staff supports the argument that such nurses are not automatically interchangeable.'

In the absence of any scientific justification for a given school of thought, the nurse's attitude to her work must be determined by a complex interaction between her own personality and beliefs, the biases of those responsible for her training, and the general atmosphere and ideology of the hospital in which she works. That attitudes to the job, once acquired, are held with considerable conviction and emotionality is a commonplace observation of those working in this field, particularly of those who have been concerned in trying to change them (see Martin's, 1962, book). Revans (1964) has argued for a greater understanding of the nurse's problems in learning and communicating in general hospitals, and there is little reason to believe that the mental nurse enjoys any greater freedom in this respect. There is no such thing as a 'trained nurse' pure and simple: the nurse brings much more to the job than the application of a number of standard skills. Her attitudes and beliefs, quite apart from more basic personality characteristics, will also determine her approach to the basic task; and, indeed, it has been felt necessary to give such considerations as these a good deal of weight in the selection of nurses for some of the units involved in the present study. It is possible that measures of relevant attitudes, such as that discussed above, may be of some value in rationalizing selection procedures, as well as in providing an estimate of the effect of training programmes.

ATTITUDES OF PATIENTS

In all, eighty-two patients were included in the principal components analysis, drawn from four different hospitals. All the patients had spent some time in, or were about to be discharged from, acute admission wards or neurosis units in these hospitals at the time of completing the questionnaire. Patients answered the questionnaire entirely voluntarily, and the anonymity of their replies was guaranteed—this led, in fact, to the unfortunate result that a good deal of useful information was lost, such as age, sex and diagnosis of some of the respondents. Only patients considered by their doctors to be too dull or out of touch to be co-operative were not asked to complete the questionnaire.

Relevant data concerning patients from the four hospitals are summarized in table 9 (p. 80).

All but six of the patients in hospital A were drawn from a neurosis unit which is run on therapeutic community lines, with virtually no physical treatments being given. Hospital B is a large mental hospital run largely on conventional lines, though at the time the patients answered the questionnaire an attempt was being made to introduce some aspects of therapeutic community practice on some of the admission wards. Hospital C is a modern unit primarily for the treatment of neurosis, again run largely as a therapeutic community, but with extensive use of physical treatments. Hospital D is an acute admission hospital dealing with a specific 'catchment area'. All the patients in this hospital were receiving therapeutic community treatment, with no patient receiving exclusively physical treatment, although a number were on drugs and a smaller number were receiving electro-convulsive therapy.

As before, the first three components yielded by the principal components analysis of the patients' scores will be considered. Table 10 (p. 81) shows the relevant data concerning questionnaire items on the normalized components, set out as before with latent roots and the percentage of variance accounted for by each.

TABLE 9. COMPOSITION OF SAMPLE OF PATIENTS

	Hospital			
	A	B	C	D
No. of patients	23	16	21	22
Age				
Mean	29	33	31	
Range	17–49	18–60	18–54	
Not known	1	4	–	22*
Sex				
Male	10	6	11	
Female	12	10	10	
Not known	1	–	–	22*
Diagnosis				
Neurotic	17	4	16	
Psychotic	4	2	1	
Psychopath/addiction	2	3	3	
Epileptic/organic	–	2	1	
Not known	–	5	–	22*

* It is only known with this sample that, in terms of sex, age and diagnosis, it approximates to the average admissions of any mental hospital.

Once again component 1 bears a close resemblance to the first components extracted in the other two samples; the emphasis here is, at the positive pole, on the effectiveness (for the better) of physical treatment, the need for hygiene and strict discipline, and for maintaining nurses and doctors in an idealized, omnipotent and unapproachable position. A positive effort should be made to avoid discussion of disturbing problems, and interpersonal relations on the ward should be purely formal. Thus high positive scores on this component suggest that mental illness is seen solely in physical terms, with the setting in which it is treated conforming closely to the stereotype of the regimented general hospital ward.

The positive pole of component 2 in this sample stresses the therapeutic value of close relationships and frank communication be-

TABLE 10. QUESTIONNAIRE ITEMS WITH A SATURATION OF AT LEAST ±0·15 ON EACH COMPONENT FOR THE PATIENT SAMPLE

	Questionnaire items		
	Component 1	*Component 2*	*Component 3*
	8 (+)	3 (+)	5 (+)
	11 (+)	4 (+)	7 (+)
	16 (+)	7 (−)	12 (+)
	17 (+)	10 (+)	13 (+)
	27 (+)	13 (+)	17 (+)
	28 (+)	25 (+)	30 (+)
	29 (+)	30 (−)	33 (−)
	34 (+)	31 (+)	42 (+)
	38 (+)	32 (+)	45 (+)
	39 (+)	43 (+)	48 (−)
	40 (+)	52 (+)	54 (+)
	44 (+)	55 (+)	62 (+)
	51 (+)	58 (+)	65 (−)
	53 (+)	60 (+)	67 (+)
	71 (+)	63 (+)	69 (−)
	74 (+)	65 (+)	72 (+)
		66 (+)	73 (+)
		76 (+)	
Latent root	10·32	5·08	3·90
Per cent variance	13·76	6·78	5·20

tween staff and patients, i.e. the reduction of 'psychological distance'. In contrast to component 1, the patient is seen as being helped in the last analysis only by someone who is personally concerned about him. The 'traditional' doctor's role comes in for heavy criticism, and nurses are considered to have an equally, if not more, important role in therapy. Despite appearances to the contrary, it should, of course, be borne in mind that components 1 and 2 here are not negatively related, indeed are not related at all.

As with the psychiatrist and nurse samples, component 3 is

more difficult to interpret. Here again the reduction of psychological distance is seen as helpful; for example, it is felt that patients are helped most by people they can regard as individuals rather than as professional workers, although there is a heavy reliance on the doctor as an all-powerful, if benevolent, source of superior knowledge, with the nurses playing a relatively minor role. Also stressed, however, is the positive contribution which the patient himself must make to his recovery—treatment is seen as disturbing and painful, with recovery dependent on the patient actually trying out new ways of feeling and behaving. Thus, in contrast to component 2, where a greater 'blurring of roles' is emphasized, high positive scores on component 3 might be considered to be related more to 'traditional' group therapy than to therapeutic community philosophy.

Comparison of patients' attitudes between hospitals

It seems likely that patients' attitudes to treatment will to a large extent be derived from the setting in which they receive it. In order to substantiate this argument we examined the scores of sixty-six patients, which were available from the computer analysis, on each of the three components. The mean scores on these components for each of the four hospitals are shown in table 11.

TABLE 11. MEAN SCORES OF PATIENTS ON COMPONENTS 1, 2 AND 3 FOR HOSPITALS A, B, C AND D

	Hospital A (N=17)		Hospital B (N=15)		Hospital C (N=13)		Hospital D (N=21)	
	Mean	*S.D.*	*Mean*	*S.D.*	*Mean*	*S.D.*	*Mean*	*S.D.*
Component 1	−1·83	2·04	1·04	2·13	2·47	3·11	−1·14	3·72
Component 2	0·19	1·52	−0·03	2·29	−1·16	2·06	1·03	1·97
Component 3	1·08	1·39	−2·17	2·09	0·61	1·56	−0·04	1·57

Analyses of variance show that significant differences between the mean scores of patients from the four hospitals emerge on all three components (on component 1 $F = 6{\cdot}65$, $p < 0{\cdot}001$; on component 2 $F = 3 \cdot 19$, $p < 0 \cdot 05$; on component 3 $F = 10 \cdot 82$, $p < 0 \cdot 001$). Even allowing for the effects of uncontrolled variables such as sex and age, this suggests that the institution may to a large extent condition the patient's attitude to his illness and the appropriate treatment for it. Table 12 summarizes the significant differences between the hospitals, based on t tests following the F test, with the hospitals listed according to descending order of mean scores for each component.

TABLE 12. SIGNIFICANT DIFFERENCES BETWEEN MEAN SCORES ON COMPONENTS 1, 2 AND 3 FOR PAIRED HOSPITALS

	Hospitals (in descending order of mean scores)	*Significant differences*
Component 1	C, B, D, A	
	C–B	n.s.
	D–A	n.s.
	B–D	n.s.
	C–D	$t = 2 \cdot 78$, $p < 0 \cdot 01$
	B–A	$t = 3 \cdot 73$, $p < 0 \cdot 001$
	C–A	$t = 4 \cdot 34$, $p < 0 \cdot 001$
Component 2	D, A, B, C	
	D–A	n.s.
	B–C	n.s.
	A–B	n.s.
	D–B	n.s.
	A–C	n.s.
	D–C	$t = 2 \cdot 96$, $p < 0 \cdot 01$
Component 3	A, C, D, B	
	A–C	n.s.
	D–B	$t = 3 \cdot 33$, $p < 0 \cdot 01$
	C–D	n.s.
	A–D	$t = 2 \cdot 20$, $p < 0 \cdot 05$
	C–B	$t = 3 \cdot 71$, $p < 0 \cdot 002$
	A–B	$t = 4 \cdot 92$, $p < 0 \cdot 001$

Differences on component 1 are roughly in accord with what one would expect from a knowledge of the use made in the different hospitals of physical treatments. On component 2 it appears that hospital D has been more successful in communicating therapeutic community attitudes to the patients than have the other hospitals. Since it lays claim to an advanced stage of therapeutic community development, and can be regarded historically as a pioneer of this method of treatment, it is of interest that hospital A, in comparison to hospital D, has a lower mean score on this component, and is not significantly different from any of the others. On the other hand, hospital A is highest on component 3, which appears to represent more the doctor-centred, group therapy approach. Thus, bearing in mind the findings with the other samples in this chapter, although medical staff tend to express clearly identifiable attitudes concerning their orientation to treatment, in some therapeutic communities the treatment philosophy is either not always successfully communicated to patients and nurses, or is only partially put into practice.

However these considerations may be, this particular measure of patients' attitudes to treatment may have useful application in determining the extent to which treatment programmes are understood and assimilated by patients. Again, the interaction between the orientation of those who carry out the treatment and the attitudes towards it of those who receive it may have important implications for both morale and prognosis. These would be obvious lines for further inquiry.

In the minds of those who treat the mentally ill, opinion fills the vacuum created by lack of knowledge. In this process medical opinion probably sets the pace, and medical opinion is founded on assumptions, beliefs, prejudices, and rare, precariously established scraps of empirically derived fact. It is probably true that in most mental hospitals the senior medical staff determine to a large extent the basic therapeutic atmosphere, if only indirectly; and it has been demonstrated above that from hospital to hospital this atmosphere can differ radically and results in attitudes which are diametrically opposed. Nursing staff display similar expressions of opinion, and the fact that an examination of their views can to a considerable extent identify the institution in which they work suggests the influence of a hospital culture often, if not always and if not completely, reflecting the prevailing medical attitude. Cohen and Struening (1964) have also indicated that the policies of those higher in the hospital hierarchy may have a great influence on the attitudes of those lower down the scale. It might be argued that the influence of doctors on the attitudes of nurses will be felt most strongly where contact between nurses and doctors is most frequent, and that, where this is poor, the nurse-patient relationships will be determined more by the communication structure within the nursing hierarchy itself; this is again reminiscent of Revans' (1964) findings. These are undoubtedly important factors in need of detailed study. Nevertheless, the fact that, in the hospitals we have studied, the opinion of nurses is in many respects related to the attitudes of the senior doctors suggests that the doctors' influence may be brought to bear indirectly through participation in the selection of certain key figures such as nursing tutors, matrons and chief male nurses. That patients should also reflect the prevailing views of the institution to which they are admitted is scarcely surprising, even though it may signify a rather passive view of their own difficulties. But they are told that such is their illness and such is the treatment, and in a cultural setting in which 'science' is magic and doctors are among its chief practitioners, they can scarcely be blamed for accepting these beliefs, whether or not they coincide with their own experience.

The question of how far expressed attitudes are actually put into practice, as opposed to being merely reiterated by those who come into contact with the institutional philosophy, is one for further research. However, some tangential evidence concerning this problem does exist. Cohen and Struening (1962, 1963, 1964), in a large-scale operation involving thousands of mental hospital employees, established a questionnaire concerning opinions towards mental illness with which they were able to identify hospital atmosphere. This instrument differed from our own in that it tapped general attitudes towards the mentally ill of a kind which one might perhaps expect to meet in the lay population (e.g. authoritarian and restrictive—patients should be locked up away from the general public; benevolent 'kindly paternalism'; the view that mental illness is 'an illness like any other'). With this instrument they were able to establish that institutions characterized by the authoritarian-restrictive atmosphere were less 'effective' than others, in that they were less successful in returning patients to the community during a period of six months to one year after admission. (This criterion of effectiveness seems somewhat doubtful, indeed circular, in view of the fact that, in restricting their patients in this way, these hospitals were doing little more than practising what they preached.) In a study making use of Cohen and Struening's questionnaire, Ellsworth (1965) found that patients actually perceived both authoritarian *and* benevolent nursing staff as cold, aloof and belittling. Thus the benevolent attitude was not reflected in the patients' experience, but appeared to cover up a patronizing and placating attitude designed to secure a quiet life for the member of staff. As it happened, patients perceived as most helpful those nurses who rejected all traditional attitudes towards the mentally ill and who appeared as the result to be treating the patients as people on the same level as themselves. An analogy with this finding might be our own results with the sample of doctors discussed earlier: only those who scored low on component 1 (probably the least 'traditional' of all) appear not to hold a rather omnipotent and controlling view of their role in treatment.

We do not regard the research reported in this chapter as in any way finished or conclusive. These are small beginnings, in which we are provided with a set of broadly constructed pigeon-holes into which we can slot the attitudes of staff and patients for further comparison and analysis. We have some sort of normative data which may serve as a starting-point for studies of greater depth in which the significance of the single case may be more closely examined.

If nothing else, we hope we have done something towards shattering the illusion of unanimity and infallibility which the profession so often offers for public consumption.

CHAPTER 5

The personalities of psychiatrists

In the last chapter we raised the question of how far the attitudes to treatment uncovered by our questionnaire may be related to more basic personality characteristics of the respondents. This is, of course, only one aspect of the problem involved in explaining the attitude constellations we have identified—playing an equal, if not greater role, would be such factors as training and experience, the influence of the individual on the institution in which he works, the effects on attitude formation of communications and morale, and so on. Nevertheless, in the selection and training of doctors personality factors are rarely, if ever, taken into account to any significant extent; and to determine whether they have any part to play in the subsequent activities of psychiatrists seems, to us at least, to be a matter of great interest. It is with this question that we shall be concerned in this chapter.

It is at least arguable that the attitudes and beliefs concerning treatment for the mentally ill current in any particular institution (and we have already seen that such attitudes seem to be fairly uniform *within*, though not *between* institutions) are set primarily by the medical staff, most probably by the consultant psychiatrists. It is for this reason that we have chosen to examine the personalities of doctors rather than of other members of staff.

From arguments presented earlier in the book it should by now be abundantly clear why we feel such an undertaking to be necessary, or even interesting in the first place. It is, of course, true that, in considering the activities of the members of most professions, it would scarcely be felt relevant to start by examining their personality characteristics. But psychiatry is almost unique among professions in that the activities of its members are not determined by an established body of knowledge which they may learn and apply—whether successfully or unsuccessfully, and whether that knowledge is established empirically (as in the natural sciences) or formally (as in the legal professions). In psychiatry, what the practitioner chooses to believe and the way in which he chooses to treat his patients are very largely up to him, and this allows his personality characteristics a very wide sphere of influence.

We are not alone in recognizing the importance of this issue, nor are we the first to subject it to empirical investigation; but for the purposes of this discussion we shall present our own research findings first, before we examine some of the results and opinions of other workers. Our own work constitutes a pilot experiment concerning the relation between psychiatrists' attitudes as measured by the questionnaire described in the previous chapter and personality characteristics, again measured primarily by questionnaire. In fact, both the approach we have taken and the findings which have resulted from it bear a striking resemblance to a survey conducted by Kreitman (1962). This similarity is all the more impressive because we were ignorant of Kreitman's results at the time of completing our research—this is, of course, not a matter about which one would normally boast, but in this case it has led to the fortunate outcome that we have confirmed a set of results, our ignorance of which made it impossible for us to have formed any preconceptions about what we should be looking for.

THE INSTRUMENTS USED

As the measure of attitude to treatment, we decided to use scores on component 1 of our questionnaire. The reasons for this were that these scores, as far as the psychiatrist sample is concerned, had given us the best differentiation between doctors of different types of orientation, and in particular between 'organic' and 'therapeutic community' doctors. Component 1, moreover, has appeared with reasonable consistency in all three samples tested (i.e. doctors, nurses and patients), and thus appears to be the most stable measure of attitude. We should perhaps repeat that high scores on this component represent emphasis on physical treatments, formal role-relationships, strict discipline, concealment by staff of their own emotional responses and personality characteristics, and acceptance of the absolute authority of the doctor. Low scores tend to represent the *opposite* of these views. Organic, physical treatment psychiatrists score highest, and therapeutic community psychiatrists lowest.

As the main measure of personality the Cattell 16-PF test was used (Cattell and Eber 1957). This consists of a questionnaire of 187 items, and measures sixteen personality factors which have been arrived at after extensive factor-analytic research. These factors are characterized by Cattell as follows (the description on the left refers always to *lower* scores):

A Reserved *v.* outgoing (syzothymia *v.* affectothymia)
B Less intelligent *v.* more intelligent (lower *v.* higher scholastic mental capacity)
C Affected by feelings *v.* emotionally stable (lower *v.* higher ego strength)
E Humble *v.* assertive (submissiveness *v.* dominance)
F Sober *v.* happy-go-lucky (desurgency *v.* surgency)
G Expedient *v.* conscientious (weaker *v.* stronger superego strength)
H Shy *v.* venturesome (threctia *v.* parmia)
I Tough-minded *v.* tender-minded (harria *v.* premsia)
L Trusting *v.* suspicious (alaxia *v.* protension)
M Practical *v.* imaginative (praxernia *v.* autia)
N Forthright *v.* shrewd (artlessness *v.* shrewdness)
O Placid *v.* apprehensive (untroubled adequacy *v.* guilt proneness)
Q_1 Conservative *v.* experimenting (conservatism *v.* radicalism)
Q_2 Group dependent *v.* self-sufficient (group adherence *v.* self-sufficiency)
Q_3 Undisciplined self-conflict *v.* controlled (low integration *v.* high self-concept control)
Q_4 Relaxed *v.* tense (low ergic tension *v.* high ergic tension)

As is true of all factor-analytic studies, the names Cattell has given these factors represent his own interpretation of them, and one should not be misled into believing that they give a necessarily accurate picture of the underlying dimensions which go to make them up. In fact, a representative of what Cattell has called an 'over-ripe' culture (meaning, presumably, European as opposed to North American) might well feel that he could provide more apt names for the factors. Cattell has himself suggested a way round this problem by giving the factors numbers in a 'universal index', but this scientistic contrivance need not concern us greatly here. Suffice it to note that neither the 'simpler descriptive labels' nor the 'technical names used by the professional psychologist' (i.e. the names given in parentheses above, in many cases neologisms devised by Cattell and his colleagues) need be thought of as adequate descriptions of the underlying personality traits.

As a further, experimental, measure of personality we decided to use an adaptation of the repertory grid technique, originally invented by Kelly (1955), and further elaborated in this country by Bannister (1965). This technique provides a concealed method of determining the way an individual 'construes' his interpersonal environment by measuring the degree of correlation between different attitudes (or 'constructs') he may hold. From this we derived six scores for each psychiatrist, as follows:

Score	*Method of measurement* (Degree of relationship between two constructs)
1. Ambition	People I would like to be like in character People likely to become widely known and respected in their profession
2. Materialism	People like me in character People likely to value material success
3. Value of relationships	People I would like to be like in character People able to establish warm relationships and empathize with others
4. Authoritarianism	People I would like to be like in character People who would be able to give firm and decisive leadership

5.	Democratic	People I would like to be like in character
		People who have a democratic outlook
6.	Social ambition	People I would value as personal friends
		People of high social status

These scores were chosen on the basis of our feelings about the kind of personality attitudes which might lie behind preference for, say, a therapeutic community approach to treatment as against an organic, physical treatment approach. Doctors were asked to rank four junior and four senior psychiatrists known to them personally on each of the constructs. Their score is derived from the Spearman correlation coefficient between whichever of the two rankings is in question. In fact, this approach was unfortunate on at least two counts: first, in asking for four junior and four senior psychiatrists we had built into the test a dimension that could only confuse the issue and which we could not directly keep track of; and secondly, there is very little guarantee that different individuals will interpret the constructs in the same way, or, indeed, that they will even find them relevant to their own way of seeing people. Indeed, we have ourselves shown that to provide a standard set of constructs to different people may invalidate the usefulness of the test (Caine and Smail 1967*b*).

THE SAMPLE

Fifty-one doctors who had taken part in the attitude study were contacted and asked to assist us in the personality research—the criterion for their selection was that we knew their names and addresses, and that they were of British extraction or education (so that cultural variables would be minimized). Of these, thirty-five agreed to co-operate. Thus the final sample of thirty-five represents a 69 per cent response rate. Quite clearly this is in no way a randomly selected sample, but one comprising a particularly co-operative group.

Of the thirty-five members of the sample, twenty-one were senior doctors (senior registrar or above), and fourteen were junior doctors (junior registrar or below), twenty-eight were male and seven female.

HYPOTHESES

Predictions of doctors' scores on the 16-PF test were arrived at by considering the individual items which go to make up the various factors, and by deciding how those with high scores on component I of the attitude questionnaire would answer them when compared with those with low scores. It became apparent during this exercise that quite often we were predicting that those with low scores on component I (i.e. therapeutic community doctors) would score at the 'pathological end' of some of the 16-PF factors (e.g. factor C–lower ego strength). The reason for this was our feeling that doctors who scored low on component I would be more sensitive to items of this kind, and *more likely to admit* feelings that might be thought to cast them in an unfavourable light than the more organically oriented doctor, rather than that they are *in fact* more 'neurotic'. The specific predictions arrived at for each of the sixteen factors were as follows:

Factor	Prediction
A, B	No difference between high and low scorers on component I
C, E, F, G	Low scorers on component I to score lower
H	No difference between high and low scorers on component I
I, L, M	Low scorers on component I to score higher
N	Low scorers on component I to score lower
O, Q_1, Q_2	No difference between high and low scorers on component I
Q_3	Low scorers on component I to score lower
Q_4	No difference between high and low scorers on component I

In addition to the sixteen 'first-order' factors above, Cattell has described three 'second-order' factors—introversion–extraversion, anxiety, and neuroticism. Since scores on the first-order factors determine scores on the second-order factors, so our predictions concerning the former were able to a large extent to determine our predictions concerning the latter. These were as follows:

Neuroticism	Low scorers on component 1 to score higher (i.e. more 'neurotic')
Anxiety Extraversion	No difference between high and low scorers on component 1

Predictions concerning the repertory grid scores were also made:

Ambition Materialism	Low scorers on component 1 to score lower
Value of relationships	Low scorers on component 1 to score higher
Authoritarianism	Low scorers on component 1 to score lower
Democratic	Low scorers on component 1 to score higher
Social ambition	Low scorers on component 1 to score lower

RESULTS

In order to test hypotheses concerning the 16-PF test, we divided the sample of thirty-five doctors into two groups according to their scores on component 1. This we achieved by splitting the sample at the median, with the case falling at the median being dropped to give two equal groups of seventeen high scorers and seventeen low scorers. Table 13 shows the mean scores on each of the sixteen personality factors of these two groups, together with t ratios for the significance of the differences between the groups (tests of significance were not carried out where the difference between the means of the two groups was clearly negligible).

The results for the three second-order factors—anxiety, extraversion and neuroticism—of the 16-PF test are shown in table 14.

Scores on the repertory grid test, for each of the six variables, range in principle from $+100$ to -100, and even a cursory glance shows that they are not normally distributed; for this reason comparisons on these scores between those who scored high on component 1 and those who scored low were effected by means of a median test. One doctor out of the original sample of thirty-five had

TABLE 13. MEAN SCORES OF HIGH AND LOW SCORERS ON COMPONENT I ON SIXTEEN PERSONALITY FACTORS, AND SIGNIFICANT DIFFERENCES BETWEEN THE TWO GROUPS

	Personality factors															
	A	B	C	E	F	G	H	I	L	M	N	O	Q_1	Q_2	Q_3	Q_4
	High scorers															
Mean	5·29	9·18	6·24	6·35	4·76	4·76	4·76	5·88	4·47	6·18	4·18	4·94	7·00	6·41	4·18	5·41
S.D.	1·77	0·99	2·37	2·22	1·16	2·26	2·10	2·54	2·09	1·82	2·01	1·44	1·53	2·14	1·04	2·35
	Low scorers															
Mean	5·71	9·24	4·59	5·88	5·41	3·06	4·71	7·41	5·53	6·53	3·29	5·88	6·59	5·41	4·06	6·53
S.D.	2·22	1·00	2·45	1·64	1·68	1·21	1·74	1·54	1·76	1·46	2·11	1·53	2·03	2·57	1·51	1·85
t	–	–	1·93	–	1·26	2·65	–	2·06	1·55	–	1·21	1·79	–	–	–	–
p	n.s.	n.s.	<0·05*	n.s.	n.s.*	<0·01*	n.s.	<0·025*	<0·10*	n.s.	n.s.*	n.s.†	n.s.	n.s.	n.s.	n.s

* one-tail test † two-tail test

not completed the repertory grid, and so the total sample here consists of thirty-four. In fact, in only one of the six comparisons is there a statistically significant result, and this is for the grid measure of 'social ambition', low scorers on component 1 being

TABLE 14. MEAN SCORES OF HIGH AND LOW SCORERS ON COMPONENT 1 ON THE THREE SECOND-ORDER FACTORS OF THE 16-PF, AND SIGNIFICANT DIFFERENCES BETWEEN THE TWO GROUPS

		Anxiety	Extraversion	Neuroticism
High scorers	Mean	5·35	4·94	4·76
	S.D.	1·97	1·98	2·18
Low scorers	Mean	6·59	5·06	6·47
	S.D.	1·91	1·47	1·72
	t	1·80	–	2·06
	p	<0·10 (two-tail)	n.s.	<0·01 (one-tail)

significantly less 'socially ambitious' than high scorers ($\chi^2 = 5{\cdot}24$, $p < 0{\cdot}01$ on a one-tail test). Thus for those who scored high on component 1, the construct 'people I would value as personal friends' shows a higher positive relationship with the construct 'people of high social status' than is true of those who scored low on component 1.

As far as age, sex and status (junior or senior rank) are concerned, there are no significant differences between the high and low scorers on component 1.

DISCUSSION

Of the original nineteen hypotheses concerning the 16-PF test, thirteen were supported (concerning factors A, B, C, G, H, I, O, Q_1, Q_2, Q_4, and anxiety, extraversion and neuroticism), five were in the correct direction but were not statistically significant (factors E, L, M, N and Q_3), and one was in the wrong direction, though again not statistically significant (factor F). As far as the repertory grid test was concerned, only one of the six hypotheses was supported—that concerning 'social ambition'.

The objections to the form of the repertory grid used here (which were mentioned earlier) make the results with this instrument hard to interpret and hence of no very great value. One cannot know how different doctors were interpreting the construct 'people of high social status'; and in any case the 'finding' that doctors who scored high on component 1, compared to those who scored low, prefer their friends to have this advantage is of little practical value. That there are no differences between the two groups on the more pertinent scores, such as authoritarianism and democratic outlook, is a more serious indication that the test misfired (this seems a more likely explanation, when one bears in mind that component 1 itself reflects very much these attitudes, and in view of the known objections to this form of the grid, than that there really are no differences in these respects between the groups).

The findings with the 16-PF test are more encouraging. On this instrument, high scorers on component 1 (characterized by the psychiatrist oriented towards physical treatments) compared to the low scorers (characterized by the therapeutic community psychiatrist) may be seen as more 'emotionally stable' (factor C), more 'conscientious' (factor G), more 'tough-minded' (factor I), and less 'neurotic' (second-order factor of neuroticism). One way to interpret these findings would be to suggest that the 'organic' psychiatrist is more reliable and realistic, and generally better adjusted than his therapeutic community colleague. Another would be to suggest that he is more hidebound, and less sensitive and insightful. As mentioned earlier, when making our predictions concerning these variables, we felt that, simply because of the kind of orientation to treatment they subscribed to, the low scorers on component 1 would be more likely to admit to elements in their character which the more diagnostically-minded psychiatrist would dismiss as pathological and hence find difficult to apply to himself. It should also be borne in mind that as far as the norms of the 16-PF test are concerned (where the average score, or 'sten', on any given factor is 5·5 and where, to quote Cattell and Eber, 1957, 'Only when we get to stens of 4 and 7 do we think of a person definitely departing from the average'), the extent of the scores shown on the factors in question by the low scorers on component 1 cannot be considered by any means grossly deviant. Considered overall, in fact, the differences between the two groups are relatively slight, and it certainly would not be possible to use the 16-PF as a means of *identifying* psychiatrists of different orientations—for this the attitude questionnaire described in the last chapter would seem very much more appropriate. To say that the differences are slight, however, is not to say that they are unimportant.

The present pilot investigation does little more than raise some interesting questions: for instance, we still do not know how much the discriminating personality traits are primary, and how much they are the consequence of experience and training, though one would certainly suspect, in view of the fact that many of the respondents were of relatively senior status, that in some cases at least personality factors may play a major role in determining the psychiatrist's choice of orientation.

Perhaps the greatest value of the present study is the confirmation it provides for Kreitman's (1962) findings. His very thorough study, mentioned earlier in this chapter, merits discussion at some length. Kreitman developed an attitude scale contrasting the organic, or 'O' orientation, with the psychoanalytic, interpersonal, or 'A' orientation. Although this tended to be an *a priori* rather than an empirically derived scale, it may be compared, perhaps, to the two poles of our component 1, and discriminated successfully between psychiatrists who in fact characterized these two types of orientation. 'O' and 'A' scores were then related to scores on the Guilford–Martin Personality Inventory, and to the two underlying factors of the Minnesota Multiphasic Personality Inventory (MMPI), i.e. the 'A' factor, representing anxiety, and the 'R' factor, representing an expressive-repressive dimension. Also used was a rating scale of introversion–extraversion provided by a Jungian analyst and developed according to Jung's criteria for this dimension, i.e. direction of interest rather than merely degree of sociability. The age and status of the respondents were taken into account, as were the length of their post-graduate, but pre-psychiatric training, and details of the duration and place of their psychiatric training and practice. Respondents approached were the entire clinical staff of the Maudsley and Bethlem Hospitals, excluding those with less than three months training as well as those who were neither British nor North American. In all, seventy-eight doctors took part. The correlation between the 'O' and 'A' attitudes was −0·64—Kreitman maintains, curiously enough, that this confirms that the two attitudes are sufficiently distinct to be measured separately and yet are not necessarily antithetical, whereas it would seem to us that one could equally well maintain that they represent opposite poles of a single dimension.

The application of median tests to his data revealed the following results: on the Guilford–Martin Inventory, high (versus low) 'A' scorers showed significantly greater 'thinking introversion' and 'depression', and also scored significantly higher when the 'depression' and 'cycloid' scales were considered together. High 'A' scorers also showed greater anxiety on the MMPI and were significantly more introverted on the Jungian rating scale. The only significant finding for high (versus low) 'O' scorers was a lower score on the 'thinking introversion' scale of the Guilford–Martin Inventory. With increasing experience in psychiatry there is an increase in 'A' scores, while greater post-graduate, non-psychiatric experience tends to result in lower 'A' scores. The critical time for an increased adoption of an 'A' attitude appears to be between one and a half and two to three years of experience in psychiatry. Kreitman suggests that it is quite feasible that experience in psychiatry should affect personality scores as well as scores on the 'O' and 'A' scales.

What is particularly striking about this study is the finding, similar to our own, that the psychodynamic, high 'A' scorers show greater depression and anxiety, and hence may be regarded as being more neurotic than psychiatrists who subscribe to a less 'psychological' viewpoint. Kreitman also finds himself unable to decide whether this is a sign of greater pathology or of greater insight, though if anything he seems to favour the latter view. Halmos (1965) has suggested that, if they are to help their patients effectively, psychotherapists should not be too 'normal', and that at least a degree of 'neuroticism' may be necessary for them to achieve a sufficient degree of empathy.

Holt and Luborsky (1958), in their exhaustive search for predictors of success in psychiatry (to be understood in this case largely as psychoanalytically oriented psychiatry), quote the words of Karl Menninger on the importance in the first place of the psychiatrist's personality (p. 259): 'The psychiatrist as a person is more important than the psychiatrist as a technician or scientist. What he *is* has more effect upon his patients than anything he *does*. Because of the intimate relationship between patient and psychiatrist, the value system, standards, interests and ideals of the doctor become very important. . . . These are for the most part characteristics of the man before he has even gone to medical school. Even those who have been selected, however, should be reminded frequently of this elementary fact, that their effectiveness as therapists depends in large part upon the stature and breadth of their own personalities.'

The task Holt and Luborsky set themselves was to try to find measures to apply to potential psychiatrists as they entered training, which would predict how successful in their profession they would prove to be. The emphasis in measurement was as much on interviews and 'projective' tests as on the more 'objective' techniques such as personality inventories. Among the most important variables which correlated with evaluations of overall competence, as judged by the trainees' supervisors, were ratings of genuineness (as opposed to facade), social adjustment with colleagues, and freedom from status-mindedness. These, if anything, appear to have more in common with the negative pole of component 1 of our own attitude scale, and perhaps also with Kreitman's 'A' scale, than with the personality measures such as the 16-PF that we have discussed above; and that they were qualities considered by psychoanalytically oriented psychiatrists to be suitable for trainees in the same discipline need not surprise us. It also seems likely that they reflect basic attitudes and value judgments rather than any ultimate evaluation of psychiatric worth. It is none the less interesting to find such attributes once again emphasized by 'dynamically' oriented psychiatrists.

Also of some relevance to the present discussion is the work of Walton (1966) and Walton and Hope (1967). From a study of medical practitioners (other than psychiatrists), these workers attempted to isolate personality and attitudinal factors characteristic of those doctors interested in psychiatry. The most relevant finding was the tendency of these doctors to be of the introverted thinking type, which again appears to have a good deal in common with Kreitman's finding concerning his high 'A' scorers.

The study by Caine (1964) referred to in the last chapter suggests that thinking introversion may also be a feature in the personality of nurses working in the therapeutic community (when compared to nurses in a general hospital), if it is permissible to interpret 'preference for working with ideas' on the Kuder Preference Record in this light. These nurses, it will be remembered, were also less authoritarian than their general hospital colleagues. In a study by Caine, Chick and Smail (1967) it has also been shown that occupational therapists working in the therapeutic community show greater preference for working with ideas, again as measured by the Kuder Preference Record, than occupational therapists in a general hospital.

On the whole, then, there appears to be a slight, but consistent tendency for doctors (and probably other professionals in the field of mental health) who prefer the 'dynamic', interpersonal approaches to treatment, when compared with their more organically minded colleagues, to be more introverted in their thinking, more sensitive to emotional disturbance, less conventional, and more tender-minded. Descriptions of this sort, however, can be misleading. From one point of view, a doctor of this persuasion could be characterized as comparatively liberal, insightful, sensitive and humane. From another, he might appear neurotic, unrealistic, over-sensitive, hopelessly idealistic. Until there is some reliable way of determining the effectiveness of different treatment programmes, the significance of such evaluative descriptions as these may remain obscure. However, for those who have some sort of differentiated picture of the kind of person they would prefer to treat their psychiatric disorders, these findings provide the beginnings of a basis for choice. Indeed, there are strong suggestions in the literature, which will be discussed in subsequent chapters, that the value systems and personalities involved in the therapist–patient dyad may be of overriding importance in the psychotherapeutic process.

CHAPTER 6

The effectiveness of the treatment of chronic, hospitalized neurotics by the therapeutic community technique

Having described the theoretical principles underlying the therapeutic community method of psychotherapy and provided some measures of the beliefs, attitudes and personality characteristics of the practitioners, an attempt at evaluation of the treatment must now be made.

Some of the difficulties associated with such an evaluation have already been discussed, and others will be mentioned in subsequent chapters. Despite these difficulties, we would argue that we have gone some way in meeting the standard criticisms of many published 'outcome of psychotherapy' research designs. The requirements for an adequate research design may be enumerated:

a. The treatment conditions, including the beliefs and attitudes of the therapists, must be defined.
b. A control or comparative treatment group comparable to the experimental group in terms of diagnosis, chronicity, severity of illness, age, etc., must be provided.
c. Samples must be representative.
d. There must be objective measures of psychological change.
e. An adequate criterion of improvement must be stipulated.
f. Patients must be followed up.

The study here described is an extension of that reported elsewhere by Caine (1965). The framework of psychological assessment in these investigations has used the distinction of three different, although related, aspects of psychological functioning, namely, *symptoms*, *personality traits* and *attitudes*. A full history of the theoretical and experimental background of this approach to assessment has been given by Foulds (1965) and Caine (in press). A somewhat briefer account may be in order here.

Certain conceptual differences can be made between these different aspects of psychological functioning, namely:

Symptoms

1. experienced as stressful
2. inhibit adjustment
3. disrupt the normal continuity of behaviour
4. experienced as alien to the personality
5. relatively transient in nature
6. may be idiosyncratic

Personality traits

1. facilitate adjustment
2. are actually *how* we behave, e.g. reacting emotionally or quickly
3. are dispositional
4. may be constitutionally determined
5. are relatively persistent in nature
6. have general application

Attitudes

1. fall somewhere between symptoms and traits
2. are not experienced as alien to the personality
3. do not represent a break in the normal continuity of behaviour
4. are not the *how* of behaviour, but are motivational
5. may be learned rather than constitutionally determined
6. have been described as enduring organizations of motivational, emotional, perceptual and cognitive processes

In these studies and in the development of the measuring instruments for the three levels of psychological functioning, we have been primarily concerned with the neuroses. In his review of the history of personality typologies Mackinnon (1944) has credited Pierre Janet, the classical expert in hysteria, with the first attempt to separate symptom complexes from personality trait constellations in the neuroses. The former were dichotomized by Janet into *psychasthenia* and *hysteria*, and the latter into *hysteroid* and *obsessoid*. *Psychasthenia* is no longer fashionable as a diagnosis, however, and we have adopted the more recent term *dysthymia* to include anxiety states, neurotic depressions and obsessive-compulsive states.

In his reviews of the literature one of the present authors (Caine 1965, in press) has found considerable support for Janet's distinctions both from the clinical and experimental points of view. Curran and Guttman (1949) state, for example, 'true obsessive-compulsive states may develop in personalities with little or no evidence of obsessional characteristics in their previous make-up', and Lewis and Mapother (1941) maintain that 'the hysterical personality ... is not found in all patients who show hysterical symptoms, but nearly all people of hysterical personality show hysterical symptoms'. Clearly a distinction is being made by these authors on clinical grounds between symptom clusters and personality trait constellations. Experimental support has come from the Slaters (1944, 1950), and more recently from Kline (1967) and Rosenberg (1967), apart from the series of studies reported by Foulds (1965) and Caine (in press) which have culminated in the measuring instruments used in the present investigation. The symptom complexes and personality trait constellations in which we are interested are shown below:

SYMPTOM COMPLEXES

Dysthymia: Unconverted disorders of feelings and moods

Anxiety

Phobias, generalized anxiety, tension and insomnia, palpitations, breathlessness, excessive perspiring, hand tremors

Neurotic depression

Loss of interest, suicidal thoughts and attempts, lack of energy, poor concentration, depressed mood, poor memory, retardation, crying

Obsessional states

Compulsions and prohibitions, excessive concern over cleanliness, distress from repetitive, pointless or obscene thoughts

Hysteria: Disorders of feelings and moods 'converted' into physical symptoms

No organic basis for: blurred vision, fits and blackouts, loss of use of some bodily part, loss of feeling in the skin, amnesia, preoccupation about physical health

DICHOTOMIZED PERSONALITY TRAIT CONSTELLATIONS

Hysteroid	*Obsessoid*
Excessive display of emotions	Scarcely any display of emotions
Vivid daydreams which come to be half believed	Complete inability to indulge in fanciful thinking
Very frequent mood changes	Mood tends to remain extremely constant
Completely lacking in conscience	Often conscience-stricken
Given to precipitate action	Slow and undecided owing to weighing of pros and cons
Childishly over-dependent	Obstinately independent
Careless and inaccurate	Stickler for precision
Emotions appear shallow	Appears to feel things deeply
Extreme desire to impress and gain attention	Extremely self-effacing

From this scheme of classification in the neuroses four categories are possible, namely, hysteria in a hysteroid personality, dysthymia in a hysteroid personality, hysteria in an obsessoid personality, and dysthymia in an obsessoid personality. In published studies by far the greatest number of neurotic patients admitted to hospital fall into the dysthymic group with the personality type split between hysteroids and obsessoids (Caine in press). There is a smaller number of hysterics with hysteroid personalities, and the smallest group is composed of hysterics with obsessoid personalities.

The first attempts to measure these different aspects of psychological functioning in juxtaposition were carried out by Foulds and Caine (1958*a*, 1959). In these studies a battery of tests composed of questionnaires, psychomotor and projective tests were administered to patients admitted to a mental hospital and clinically diagnosed as to illness and personality type. The battery of tests was then associated with the clinical assessments and, as predicted, fell into two groups. One group of tests was more closely associated with the diagnosis, the other with the personality. Since the battery was long and time-consuming, and since the questionnaires were as efficient in this classifying function as the psychomotor and projective tests, it was decided to develop special symptom and personality questionnaires specifically related to the categories in which we were interested. The construction and validation of these has been described by Foulds and Caine (Foulds 1965) and in condensed form in the test manuals (Caine and Hope 1967, Foulds and Hope 1968).

At an intermediate level a questionnaire involving several aspects of hostility and guilt was developed (Caine, Foulds and Hope 1967). This questionnaire has five subscales involving (1) acting out hostility, (2) criticism of others, (3) projected hostility, (4) self-criticism, and (5) guilt. Following the finding of Hope (1963) that the two principal components of the questionnaire were *amount of hostility* expressed and the *direction* in which it was expressed (whether inwardly or outwardly), these two measures of the test have been associated with diagnosis and personality type in a number of studies with consistent results. Total hostility is commonly associated with diagnostic category, direction with personality type. Examples of questions from the various tests related to these three areas are as follows:

SYMPTOMS: The Symptom-Sign Inventory (SSI)

Dysthymia

Anxiety state

Does your hand often shake when you try to do something?

Are there times when you feel anxious without knowing the reason?
Are you afraid of going out alone?

Neurotic depression

Have you ever attempted to do away with yourself?
Are you sometimes so low in spirits that you sit for hours on end?
Have you lost interest in almost everything?

Obsessional states

Are you unable to prevent yourself from doing quite pointless things—like tapping lampposts, touching things, counting windows, etc.?
Do you feel you have to check things again and again—like turning off taps or lights, shutting windows at night, etc.—although you know there is really no need to?
Are you excessively concerned about cleanliness?

Hysteria

Do you sometimes do things in a dream-like state without remembering afterwards what you have been doing?
Do you have fits or have difficulty keeping your balance?
Do you ever lose all feeling in any part of your skin, so that you would not be able to feel a pinprick; or do you have burning or tingling sensations under your skin?

PERSONALITY: The Hysteroid-Obsessoid Questionnaire (HOQ)

Hysteroid

When I am working I like a job which calls for speed rather than accuracy.
My conscience seldom bothers me.
I like discussing myself with other people.

Obsessoid

The opposite of the above.

ATTITUDES OF HOSTILITY AND GUILT: The Hostility and Direction of Hostility Questionnaire (HDHQ)*

Acting out hostility (AH)

I can easily make other people afraid of me and sometimes do for the fun of it.
At times I feel like smashing things.
Sometimes I enjoy hurting persons I love.

Criticism of others (CO)

I think most people would lie to get ahead.
Most people make friends because friends are likely to be useful to them.
Most people are honest chiefly through fear of being caught.

Projected hostility (PH)

I believe I am being plotted against.
I have no enemies who really wish to harm me.
If people had not had it in for me I would have been much more successful.

Self-criticism (SC)

I am certainly lacking in self-confidence.
I shrink from facing a crisis or difficulty.
My hardest battles are with myself.

Guilt (G)

I have not lived the right kind of life.
At times I think I am no good at all.
I believe my sins are unpardonable.

Although it is of interest that the clinical and research evidence is consistent with regard to the feasibility of distinguishing and measuring these different aspects of psychological functioning, the pertinent finding, as far as the present work is concerned, is a study by Foulds (1959) in which a small number of women admitted to a mental hospital and classified as neurotic were tested on the test battery described before and after six weeks of drug treatment in a conventional ward setting. Modifications were achieved in the symptom tests but not in the personality measures, and it was suggested that therapists who were dissatisfied with the mere alleviation of symptoms might try to change some of the personality measures. The implication is that changes in test measures related to symptomatology are more readily accomplished than are changes in tests related to personality traits. Therapies directed at personality reorganization and attitude change should produce more profound and enduring changes in the personality measures than should those therapies directed at symptom relief only. These changes should be more systematic and predictable than should those to be expected simply from the passage of time (Martin and Caine 1963). The study here described is a test of these hypotheses involving a comparison of the results of the treatment of neurosis in a therapeutic community with those of the treatment of neurosis in more conventional treatment settings.

THE THERAPEUTIC COMMUNITIES

The attitudes of the persons involved with therapeutic communities in terms of their treatment beliefs, staff roles, discipline, etc., have been described. The formal treatment setting, for the two therapeutic communities being assessed here, was as follows.

The units were run on the same fundamental principles, with some differences in the detail of their day-to-day organization. The larger was run as a mixed unit with a total of thirty informal patients, roughly in the proportion of one man to two women. The treatment programme extended from Monday to Friday, with the majority of the patients being encouraged to go home for the weekend. This encouragement was a part of treatment policy, in order to maintain from the start a link between the somewhat artificial atmosphere of the unit and the real-life problems of the patients' family relationships.

The medical staff of the unit consisted of a consultant psychiatrist and two registrars, all of whom worked there part time and had responsibilities in other sections of the main hospital. Their actual time in the unit would average out at two or three hours a day, although this would vary from one day to another. The nursing staff worked two shifts, with a sister or charge nurse in charge of each shift, a staff nurse on day shift, and two student nurses per shift. There was a regular night nurse, an occupational therapist and a psychiatric social worker. The latter was not full time in the unit, and her attendance was similar to that of the doctors. Thus the staff nurse and the occupational therapist were the only two members of staff who were in the unit for the whole day every day. Although these details may seem rather tedious, one suspects that they may well have a profound effect on the morale of the unit, on the emergence of loyalties, and on 'transferences' in the technical sense. Thus the limited involvement of the doctors and the psychiatric social worker, with their attendance at only the formal treatment activities, sets them apart from the rest of the community and may well give rise to fantasies of omnipotence, inscrutability, etc., on the part of the patients and, indeed in some cases, the staff. The effectiveness of this sort of relationship as a therapeutic agent in a therapeutic community, or perhaps in psychotherapy in general, is a matter of debate. What is certain is that different levels of personal involvement with the patients gives rise to a considerable amount of defensiveness, resentment and misunderstanding. This is undoubtedly an area which would prove very fertile in systematic investigation.

An essential feature of the therapeutic community is the ward meeting. In the unit being described these were held four days a week, and were attended by all staff on duty and all the patients.

Although theoretically completely free and unstructured, the staff in fact acted as a body in joining the meeting together and leaving as a group to go to the staff meeting. The senior doctor present closed the meeting and tended to be the most active member of staff, particularly in the 'making of interpretations'. The rather natural reluctance of junior staff to take a very active part in the meetings was a frequent subject of discussion in the staff meeting. Patients were encouraged to express their feelings (at least verbally) about any aspect of the unit's functioning and about any of the unit's members, whether staff or patients. The analysis of the reasons for these feelings or the behaviour which they promoted was the basic function of the ward meeting. In general, those meetings in which the patients participated most actively, both in the expression of feeling and in interpretation and analysis, were regarded as the most successful. It can be argued that the most effective psychotherapy is done by the patients themselves, with the staff acting largely as catalytic agents providing a 'safe' background for the patients' interaction. Again, however, there are disagreements and personality differences in this connection which would be a fruitful source for inquiry. The staff meeting was held immediately after the ward meeting; in it the ward meeting itself, staff tensions and differences of attitude and opinion were discussed, and information relevant to the patients' treatment was exchanged.

In addition to the ward meeting, the patients were divided into four small groups of from six to eight for more intensive group psychotherapy. Each group met twice a week with their doctor and twice a week with the occupational therapist or the staff nurse, in the mornings. Although matters of an intimate, personal nature might well be discussed in the full ward meeting, these tended, in the initial stages of a patient's treatment at least, to be discussed in the smaller groups. It is probably true that the personality of the individual doctor, staff nurse or occupational therapist would have a more decisive effect on group interaction in the smaller groups than in the ward meeting. There was a fairly constant turn-over of staff, since the registrars were in training and stayed in the unit for approximately a year, and the student nurses stayed only three or four months.

The afternoons were devoted to occupational activities, which were designed to throw into relief the patients' problems (perhaps with regard to authority, for example) rather than to be purely diversionary. Evening social activities were planned by the patients under the guidance of the nursing staff, and here again the attempt was made to give the patients the ultimate responsibility for running and organizing the function. Every month an evening community meeting was held, to which patients who had left the hospital but who felt the need for some further support were invited. On average four or five availed themselves of this opportunity, but usually only once or twice.

In addition to the formal therapeutic activities, the patients would spend a considerable amount of time discussing the unit and their own problems amongst themselves, and might be joined by a member of the nursing staff or the occupational therapist in an informal way. It would be fair to say that psychotherapeutic treatment was continuous and intensive throughout the day, and frequently during the evenings as well.

The other therapeutic community unit, from which a minority of the patients in this study came, was a unit of only twenty beds. Instead of a shift system, there was one sister in charge on spread-over duty with two student nurses on each shift. During the period under consideration there was no occupational therapist, and there were only two senior doctors. Ward meetings were held daily, but were attended by the doctors only one day a week, being otherwise conducted by the sister. The doctors were involved mainly in the smaller groups. Although the general approach was very similar for the two units, the roles of the senior staff and their relations with the patients must have varied considerably. The absence of any striking differences in the results of treatment between the two units gives some support to the view that patients' participation and interaction is of primary importance in this method of treatment.

It should be emphasized that, apart from the occasional crisis, no drugs were administered and the treatment may fairly be described as purely psychological.

THE COMPARATIVE TREATMENT

Two mental hospitals and a neurosis unit provided the patients for the comparative treatment sample. All the treatment institutions were within a radius of twenty miles from London and were within ten miles of each other, with the parent hospital of the therapeutic community units occupying a fairly central position. The catchment areas were therefore not too discrepant, although there were more patients from the rural areas around London in the therapeutic community sample than there were from the neurosis unit. It is not possible to specify precisely the amount of psychotherapy received by the comparative treatment group, although, if any, it was a great deal less than that received by the therapeutic community group, both in terms of duration and intensity. This would be inevitable because of the lower staff/patient ratio and the considerable difference in average length of stay, which varied from six weeks approximately for the comparative group to six months for the therapeutic community sample. Thus the comparative treatment group were a sample of patients admitted to these three treatment institutions in the normal course of events, as neurotics, and were administered the routine treatment programmes which were of a more conventional kind than that of the therapeutic communities. This may be described as a greater emphasis on drug treatments, a minimum psychotherapy represented by the personal relations established with a member of staff or another patient, and, in some cases, a limited amount of interpretive psychotherapy by a doctor or an experienced ward sister. The medical and nursing staff of two of the hospitals concerned scored somewhat higher on component 1 of the questionnaire measure of attitudes to treatment described in chapter 4 than did the therapeutic community staff.

SELECTION OF PATIENTS

Both the therapeutic community group and the comparative treatment sample consisted of patients diagnosed as neurotics on admission. For both groups these were, as far as administratively possible, consecutive admissions. This was certainly true of the therapeutic community group, although the psychologist responsible for testing the comparative treatment group was not *always* informed of the admission of a patient to one of the other hospitals. Within this limitation it may be stated that these were all typical cases admitted under the prevailing treatment policies of the hospitals involved, and, to this extent, were random samples as far as the research workers were concerned. The ages ranged from 19 to 60, with a mean of 34·43 (S.D. 8·63) for the therapeutic community group and 37·42 (S.D. 10·58) for the comparative treatment sample. These means are not significantly different from each other, although there are significantly more men in the therapeutic community group. A number of case histories are described at the end of this chapter.

THE PRESENT INVESTIGATION

Background

The present study is an extension of that reported elsewhere by Caine (1965). Over a period of fourteen months all the patients who entered the two therapeutic community units and stayed longer than a month were included in the study. It was considered that six weeks would be the very minimum of time required for active participation in the community. No patient scoring below the tenth centile on the Mill Hill Vocabulary Scale was considered to be suitable for this type of psychotherapy, and, where doubt arose, patients were screened from this point of view before admission. During the period eighty-six patients were admitted, and, where possible, were tested on the battery of psychological tests on admission, after six weeks of treatment, on discharge and on follow-up one year after leaving hospital. The following is a list of the relevant details:

	Treatment completed	*Number of patients*
A	Tested and followed up	48
B	Not tested at discharge	2
C	Not tested on follow-up	9
D	Did not complete hospital testing	3

Treatment not completed

E	Self-discharge within a month of admission	12
F	Transferred to other units as psychotic or psychopathic	10
G	Still in treatment at the end of the study	2

The scores of groups A and B supplied the data for the main analysis reported in the study. The symptom, personality and sex distributions of these groups were as follows:

Clinical classification	*Women*	*Men*
Dysthymics of obsessoid personality	14	22
Dysthymics of hysteroid personality	5	3
Hysterics of obsessoid personality	3	0
Hysterics of hysteroid personality	3	0

In the clinical classification the diagnosis was made by the consultant psychiatrists concerned, and the personality classification was derived from ratings of personality traits by medical, nursing, and occupational therapy staff after approximately two weeks of observation with an average of approximately seven raters per patient.

The test battery consisted of the following measures:

Symptom measures

The Personal Disturbance Scale from the SSI (not all patients completed this test, since it was at an early stage of development at the initiation of the study)

MMPI clinical scales of Hypochondriasis, Depression and Psychasthenia

HDHQ total score

The Mooney Problem Check List (an inventory of 288 problems in the areas of physical health, personality, home and family, religion, sex, occupation, and economic security)

Personality measures

The Hysteroid-Obsessoid Questionnaire (HOQ)

HDHQ direction of hostility score derived from the formula (2SC+DG)−(AH+CO+PH)

In addition to the sample of patients, a group of thirty normals (fifteen men and fifteen women) were tested on the battery twice with an interval of one year between testing sessions. In the analysis of the results, the test scores of the patients were compared with regard to testing times, success and failure as clinically determined, and with regard to the normal sample.

The main findings of the study were:

1. There were no significant changes in the symptom, attitude and trait measures among normals after an interval of one year.
2. Neurotics who were classified as 'failures' in their response to treatment at one year follow-up, changed very much less than did the 'successful' patients. 'Failure' and 'success' were defined in terms of the amount of psychiatric treatment the patients had required since leaving hospital, and how well the patients felt they were coping with their responsibilities at home or at work. On admission the main differences in levels of test score were between normals and neurotics. At follow-up, however, the main differences were between the normals and the successful neurotics on the one hand and the failed neurotics on the other. Thus test scores reflected the clinical state of the patients reasonably well.
3. The period in which most change occurred in the direction of normality was somewhere between six weeks and discharge from hospital. The length of stay varied from six weeks to approximately eighteen months with an average of six months.
4. The trait measures appeared to be more resistant to change than did the symptom measures.
5. Patients who were less intropunitive, less depressed, and who took a less nihilistic view of themselves (as measured by the Mooney Problem Check List) were more likely to show a favourable response to treatment (or to improve with the passage of time!).

In addition to test differences between the successful and unsuccessful groups, the failure group had a significantly higher number of patients diagnosed as personality disorders, either on admission or subsequently. The personality disorder group included such diagnoses as 'schizoid personality', 'personality disorder' or 'inadequate personality'. Of the patients who were transferred to other wards, three were diagnosed as schizophrenic and three as sufficiently depressed to require electro-convulsive therapy. These latter may well be regarded as psychotic depressives.

The diagnostic difference between the failure/transfer group and the successful group was highly significant statistically.

It was considered that the failure group came to be regarded by the medical staff as revealing either deep-seated personality disturbances or psychotic processes. The admission test scores gave weight to this view, suggesting that this formulation was not simply because these patients had failed to respond to the initial treatment programme. There were no significant differences in respect of age, chronicity, or length of stay in the community wards, between the success and failure groups.

The five-year follow-up—therapeutic community group

The original groups A, B and C in the list above, i.e. those followed up at one year, were again contacted five years after leaving hospital and asked to see the psychologist in an interview, either in their homes or at the hospital. Seventy-seven per cent of the original fifty-nine patients responded, and of these 63 per cent (thirty-five patients) agreed to be interviewed and tested, the remainder responding to a questionnaire asking for details as to medical, work and social history since leaving hospital. On the basis of this questionnaire or on clinical interview at follow-up the group was classified:

1.	Successful (no further treatment, working and coping with responsibilities at home)	28
2.	On some supportive treatment, i.e. drugs or outpatient psychotherapy but working or coping in the home, not as bad as when admitted	8
3.	No improvement, unable to cope or re-admitted to hospital at some point	8

4.	Suicide	1
5.	Developed Huntingdon's Chorea	1
6.	No response to follow-up letter	10
7.	Letters returned 'unable to trace'	3

Of the 'unable to trace' group one had, in fact, telephoned the charge nurse in the unit (for the address of another patient) some months before his five-year follow-up letter. He had stated that he had been well since leaving hospital, that he was working, and that he was on the point of moving to a new town some distance from London.

As compared with the clinical state at follow-up at one year, eight were thought to be worse clinically and three were improved. Seventy-four per cent were similarly classified in both the one-year and five-year follow-ups.

Table 15 shows the mean scores for the group of thirty-five patients who agreed to be tested at five-year follow-up at the various testing periods on the symptom and personality measures. Where mean scores were significantly different from the admission mean scores, these are asterisked. Since the three clinical scales of the MMPI and the Personal Disturbance Scale behaved similarly, only the MMPI Depression Scale is shown here.

The comparative treatment sample

The comparative samples were tested on the same battery of tests and at roughly the same periods of time, on average, as the therapeutic community group. Mean scores for this group are shown in table 16 and are asterisked, etc., where they are significantly different from the admission scores. The columns in table 16 correspond to the columns in table 15 as far as average time-spans are concerned. Thus column 2 of table 16 shows the mean scores for the comparative sample on discharge, which was, on average, six weeks after admission to hospital and which may be compared with column 2 of table 15. Column 3 shows a follow-up six months after leaving hospital to compare with the discharge means of the therapeutic community group shown in column 3 of table 15, and column 4 of table 16 compares with column 4 of table 15.

TABLE 15. MEAN SCORES OF A SAMPLE OF NEUROTICS TESTED ON ADMISSION, DURING TREATMENT, ON DISCHARGE, AND ON FOLLOW-UP (THERAPEUTIC COMMUNITY SAMPLE)

	Test		On admission (1)	After six weeks' treatment (2)	On discharge (3)	At first follow-up (1 year) (4)	At second follow-up (5 years) (5)
Symptom measures	MMPI Depression	N	35	30	34	33	35
		Mean	84·11	84·80	65·65§	67·30§	64·03§
		S.D.	11·87	12·98	14·41	17·91	16·22
	Total hostility	N	35	30	34	33	35
		Mean	19·40	19·97	17·09	14·42†	15·40‡
		S.D.	8·14	6·60	6·22	6·88	6·89
Personality measures	Direction of hostility	N	35	30	34	33	35
		Mean	5·68	7·43	3·35	2·88*	2·54†
		S.D.	5·50	6·26	6·90	6·06	6·63
	HOQ	N	35	30	34	33	34
		Mean	21·06	20·23	23·12	23·21*	23·15
		S.D.	6·94	6·73	5·84	6·41	6·56
	Mooney Problem C.L.	N	35	29	34	32	31
		Mean	46·06	37·57	23·18§	19·34§	21·55§
		S.D.	25·79	22·49	20·52	20·80	19·71

Different from admission scores:

* $p < 0{\cdot}05$ † $p < 0{\cdot}02$ ‡ $p < 0{\cdot}01$ § $p < 0{\cdot}001$

TABLE 16. MEAN SCORES OF A SAMPLE OF NEUROTICS TESTED ON ADMISSION, ON DISCHARGE, AND ON FOLLOW-UP (COMPARATIVE TREATMENT GROUP)

	Test		On admission (1)	On discharge (2)	At first follow-up (6 months) (3)	At second follow-up (18 months) (4)
Symptom measures	MMPI Depression	N	24	22	23	24
		Mean	79·17	72·54	73·22	68·88†
		S.D.	14·04	13·95	15·93	18·62
	Total hostility	N	24	22	23	24
		Mean	16·96	16·09	17·39	16·00
		S.D.	7·42	7·25	9·46	9·73
Personality measures	Direction of hostility	N	24	22	23	24
		Mean	6·67	4·50*	4·83	4·12
		S.D.	6·58	6·30	6·54	6·77
	HOQ	N	24	22	23	24
		Mean	20·92	20·73	21·74	21·25
		S.D.	3·90	5·34	6·04	6·06
	Mooney Problem C.L.	N	21	20	22	23
		Mean	38·05	24·10‡	18·14§	18·09‡
		S.D.	23·07	16·50	18·98	22·53

Different from admission scores:
* $p < 0·05$ † $p < 0·02$ ‡ $p < 0·01$ § $p < 0·001$

It can be seen from these results that the main hypothesis with regard to intensive psychotherapy versus more conventional treatment methods is borne out. Table 15 shows significant changes in both the symptoms and personality measures for the therapeutic community group, which are not present in the comparative treatment sample. In column 4 of table 15 changes on all tests at all levels for the therapeutic community group are shown, whereas with the comparative treatment group in the same column of table 16, only one test is modified and this at the symptom level. It may well be that the drop in depressive symptoms thus indicated is associated with supportive drug treatment. Significantly more of the comparative treatment sample were on drugs at follow-up. These changes are sustained in the therapeutic community group four years later (or five years after leaving hospital), although the basic personality measure just fails to reach significance levels because of the slightly increased spread of the scores. Previous work has shown this to be the most difficult test to modify, and in the present study, is the only one to carry significant correlations with admission test scores throughout (table 17).

TABLE 17. RETEST CORRELATIONS OF NEUROTICS ON SYMPTOM AND PERSONALITY TESTS

	Depression	Hostility	Direction of hostility	HOQ
Admission scores and				
6th week	0·63†	0·68†	0·66†	0·78†
Discharge	0·16	0·18	0·36*	0·62†
1 FU	0·16	0·08	0·44†	0·61†
2 FU	−0·12	0·37*	0·19	0·33*
Discharge scores and				
1 FU	0·40*	0·56†	0·82†	0·71†
2 FU	0·16	0·37*	0·44†	0·49†
1 FU and				
2 FU	0·74†	0·60†	0·63†	0·62†

* $p < 0{\cdot}05$ † $p < 0{\cdot}01$

It is quite reasonable that basic personality traits should not be changed with psychotherapy, but that attitudes of hostility and guilt associated with this level of psychological functioning should. Work is in progress to determine which areas covered by the HOQ are modified by psychotherapy. The hypothesis is that the modifiable aspects of basic personality as covered by the HOQ will be the emotionally expressive and the sociability areas. After treatment patients should be less inhibited socially and more willing and able to express their real feelings.

It is of great interest that changes in test score at the more basic levels are not shown on discharge, but later at follow-up. Patients often express their anxiety about leaving the protective environment of the hospital, and it is sometimes difficult to 'wean them off' even with pressure from the other patients in the ward meetings and the small groups. At follow-up a number of patients remarked that they now applied techniques for handling interpersonal friction learned in the community wards to situations outside, and that they found them effective. No doubt this accounts for an increase in self-confidence and a lowering of hostility levels, and these are reflected in lower test scores. This finding underlines the need for follow-up work, since test results obtained simply on discharge are unlikely to reflect more than a transitory state of affairs.

A further important finding for the therapeutic community units is the relative ineffectiveness of the units in coping with the personality disorders and psychotics admitted under the far from stringent methods of selection. Virtually any patient referred to the units was accepted. Had the intake been confined to neurotics, regardless of the stage of chronicity, the success rate would undoubtedly have been higher. Here it should be emphasized that the units seemed able to treat chronic neurosis and were initially set up for that purpose. One of the successes, for example, had been ill for some eighteen years and had had a wide variety of treatments before her admission. As noted above, the great majority of neurotic patients had had a previous breakdown some years before.

In interview at follow-up a number of spontaneous remarks were made about the therapeutic community and its effects:

'I saw people there like myself, and I realized that I am not so peculiar and alone as I thought. I can talk to people now; I can accept them and see that they have problems too.'

'I learned how to cope with personal differences better. My husband and I "group" each other. I was "told straight" about myself by another patient and this helped.'

'I realized that my illness was only avoiding responsibilities and that my nerves were not the real trouble. I must do it myself. I must stand up for myself.'

'I realize now that my children must work out their own destinies. Before having treatment I thought there was a right and a wrong way of doing everything, and that I knew which was which. I realized in hospital that other people saw things differently from me, and yet they could still be right. I learned this from listening to the other patients and seeing how their attitudes were affecting their relationships. I could often apply it to myself.'

'The main thing about the treatment is talking to people who understand. You don't want sympathy, you want understanding. I was definitely "told off", but it was good for me. I felt a bit out of place as I was in a younger crowd and the talk was all sex and marriage.'

'I can stand up for myself better now. I'm not so influenced by others. I don't feel I have to fall in exactly with what my wife wants. I get the odd symptom, but I can cope with it.'

'Talking, mixing with people helped me most. The contacts on the ward on an informal basis helped more than the groups. I found others had similar problems, which was a great relief. I find people more understanding now than they used to be, and I can listen more, not so selfish but I still have difficulty with managerial types.'

One repetitive theme was that it was of great help to have someone, either a neighbour or a member of the immediate family, who was able to listen, to share experiences and even to make interpretations. One woman illustrated this by remarking: 'I got up with a headache this morning and my daughter (aged 16) said, "Oh, that's just because the psychologist is coming this afternoon." She often says things like that. It's a great help.' Where this was not possible, a number of patients found someone to see them occasionally in a professional capacity. From their accounts their conversations were of a very informal kind with only very superficial interpretations of behaviour. Drugs were regarded with a certain amount of contempt as only palliative. Table 18 shows a comparison of the reasons for improvement (if any) in psychological state given by a consecutive series of patients treated in the therapeutic communities and by more conventional methods.

TABLE 18. REASONS FOR IMPROVEMENT GIVEN BY NEUROTIC PATIENTS TREATED IN TWO DIFFERENT WAYS

Reasons	Therapeutic community N = 23	Conventional treatment N = 29
Drugs	0	19
Relationships in the hospital, meeting others like oneself	15	6
Relief from responsibilities, rest, holiday	0	19
Own will-power	2	4
New job, new house, new girl friend, more help from relatives	0	5
Shock of seeing other patients	0	2
Loss of weight	0	1
Dislike of hospital	0	1
Hospital treatment of limited value or did not help	3	12

This table reflects the heavy emphasis placed by the therapeutic community patients on the beneficial effects of the relationships in hospital in contrast to the emphasis on drugs and relief from responsibilities on the part of the other group. Item 9 shows the higher morale, as far as hospitalization is concerned, of the therapeutic community sample.

On the evidence presented here we would argue that the hypotheses advanced regarding the modification of symptom and personality related tests have been sustained. In contrast to a group of patients treated by conventional methods, a group of similar patients, treated by intensive and relatively prolonged psychotherapy, have shown more extensive changes in test scores, and these have persisted over a five-year period after leaving hospital. In the previous study described above (Caine 1965) it was found that the 'failure' (and clinically more disturbed) group tended to have higher admission scores on the symptom measures. Although differences in admission score between the two groups in the present study are not significant on these measures taken separately, the fact that in every case the therapeutic community sample shows a higher mean score suggests that it may well have been the more disturbed group.

APPENDIX:

THERAPEUTIC COMMUNITY CASE MATERIAL

The following are brief accounts of some of the patients and their progress in the therapeutic communities. The description of samples of patients purely in terms of diagnosis or personality type quite leaves out of account the more 'dynamic' aspects of the patients' life experiences, which are the raw material of psychotherapy and which are the main topics of discussion in the ward meetings and small groups. It is the traumatic intensity of these, in conjunction with the patient's 'ego strength', which may define the severity of the illness and the likelihood of eventual recovery. To preserve anonymity, certain personal details have been altered or suppressed. Otherwise the general picture is presented as accurately as possible.

Mrs W., aged 30

On admission this woman was thought to be suffering from an anxiety state with phobic symptoms. She was rated as obsessoid in personality type. She described her symptoms as 'a feeling of wanting to run away from myself. It's as though a part of me is afraid of another part of me.' She had had this feeling on and off for some twenty years, but now it had reached such proportions that she could no longer cope with her feelings of panic. She often felt violently sick, and at meal-times would have to leave the table and dash outside. She was now quite unable to carry on looking after her husband and twelve-year-old son. She denied having any family difficulties in early childhood or marital problems at the moment, but she felt that having been severely punished for enuresis repeatedly at her boarding school had affected her very adversely. In fact, she had this problem until she left school. Her father had died when she was seven, her mother had married again shortly afterwards, and she had been sent off to the boarding school without any clear explanation.

After four months of treatment it was noted that she was not making much progress, and it was felt that this was due to the relationship she had formed with a much younger man in the unit. It was felt that she had developed an intense hostility towards the staff and her husband, who had, in fact, offered her a divorce. Eventually she was able to tell her group that she had been sexually assaulted as a child over a long period by one of her two brothers, and that her marital relations both in the sexual and personal aspects had been far from satisfactory. She developed an intense 'negative transference' to one of the male nurses, who she said reminded her of her husband in his obstinacy. She was able to work this out with him, and remarked that 'for the first time in my life I've been able to get really angry with someone and tell them'.

The psychodynamic features were thought to be fairly clear now, involving separation from her parents by death and later boarding school, traumatic incidents at school in connection with her enuresis, and traumatic sexual experiences with her brother. There was little doubt that her husband was now involved in her aggressive fears and fantasies, and that he was being completely rejected. She was able to work through her difficulties in some measure and was discharged after about a year in the unit. Shortly after being discharged, however, she left her husband for a short period, but she returned home and remained well, without further psychiatric help until the five-year follow-up.

Mrs B., aged 30

Length of stay in the therapeutic community: 10 months. Diagnosis: anxiety state in an obsessoid personality. She was readmitted to the therapeutic community ward during the time of the research. She had had two periods of in-patient treatment, one of which was in a therapeutic community setting and from which she discharged herself against advice. In addition she had had a year at an out-patient clinic. She complained of anxiety symptoms and panic attacks which virtually made her a prisoner at home with her mother and father. She had two sisters and three brothers, who, except for one, were all married. From her previous records it was noted that she was an uncooperative patient, that she expressed great hostility to men, thinking that they might assault her sexually, and insisted on another woman being present when being interviewed by one of the male staff. She had fantasies about being sexually assaulted by her father and felt at times that her tea might be poisoned, although she realized that this was a feeling with no basis in fact. She stayed in the unit for almost a year and her progress was very variable. She regressed, for example, to a 'childlike, sulkily aggressive' state in response to her group pressing her to deal more directly with the family in resisting the demands they were making on her. She was able to work through this and eventually became able to assert herself with her father in a reasonable way, although her fantasies about his raping and poisoning her continued. She was able to talk about these in the group eventually and was able to see the relation between the two ideas. She was discharged with a much more realistic view of herself and her relationships. At follow-up one year after discharge she was clinically rated as a failure. Although remaining outside hospital, she was having difficulty in coping and required fairly consistent supplies of drugs. At five-year follow-up, however, she had made considerable advances. She had completely weaned herself off supportive drugs, she had married and was hoping to have a baby, and she felt quite confident that she would be able to cope. She ascribed her improvement directly to her treatment in the therapeutic community, which she said 'made me a different woman'.

Mr R., aged 45

First admitted some months before the beginning of the study to an acute admission unit, with carbon monoxide poisoning following an attempt at suicide. He was described as a small, pale, tired-looking man. His talk was fluent. He was severely depressed, and he said that he tried to take his life because he was afraid of going insane. He exhibited a number of firmly held hypochondriacal delusions. Everything is stopped in his inside and his bowels have not acted for two weeks, therefore he cannot eat. Also has a closed-up feeling in his throat. There was a history of colitis and pulmonary tuberculosis for which he had been under active treatment. He was initially diagnosed as an involutional depression in a long-standing, hypochondriacally disposed individual and was regarded as a suicidal risk. After a course of six ECTs, he made a steady improvement, and he was discharged after a stay of over five months. Arrangements were made for him to be followed up psychiatrically.

He broke down again some weeks later and was re-admitted to Claybury, but this time to the therapeutic community unit. The following history was taken: the patient was the eldest of a family of four children, two girls and two boys. His mother and three of the children, including himself, contracted TB. He lost his mother at the age of five and was brought up by an aunt who lived close by. He described his father as not actually punitive, but as neglectful and a drunkard. He was told that his father did not look after his mother when she lay ill.

He remembers acutely an occasion when going to school when his father put his hand on his head and discovered lice. He found this a most distressing incident in his life.

At school he won a scholarship, but was unable to take it up because of lack of funds. His headmaster felt sorry for him and helped him to get a job in a large London store. He remarked that in those days one almost had to pay to get into these shops.

As soon as he was earning money, he went to live in digs with his eldest brother and was extremely happy. At the age of nineteen he had his first attack of tuberculosis with pain in the left side of his chest and breathlessness. He was diagnosed as suffering from nervous debility and continued on at work. His brother was also ill with TB. When Mr R. was twenty-one, there was a fire in their digs in which his brother was injured fatally.

Mr R. then lived on alone for a short while until he met and married his wife at the age of twenty-seven. She was described as 'always so kind and thoughtful towards me', and he felt that he married her for security and a home. He never really felt much love towards her. Gradually his social position improved, and he eventually became a buyer in a drapery firm.

His son was born when he was about thirty years old, and he claims he is very fond of him. He had further attacks of tuberculosis three years and one year ago, and during the second attack had to go away to a sanatorium. At this time his wife was very distant towards him, and he had been unable to resume normal marital relations with her because he felt somehow unclean still.

His present illness began ten years ago immediately following the death of a much-loved dog. He had become withdrawn and relatively friendless, and had difficulty holding his job. He had lost weight and had been sleeping poorly over this period with a greater and greater withdrawal from life as time went on.

On admission he was described as 'a talkative, superficially confident man. He complains of loss of weight and poor appetite—also poor sleeping, wakes at 3 a.m., can't get off. Depressed. He puts a brave face on and talks about his symptoms quite a lot and touched on some parts of his earlier life. He feels the treatment (therapeutic community) is not comprehensible to him and is "slowing him up". He has the usual fears of becoming a chronic patient.'

After four months in the unit, he was found to have a small duodenal ulcer and was placed on a diet. He became more depressed, and seemed less and less capable of entering into small group intensive treatment. He was thought to need electrical convulsive treatment, but he refused it. Psychotherapy was in fact abandoned as the main course of treatment, and he was discharged following a course of librium and tofranil.

On discharge he was thought to have made considerable, rapid progress on this combination of drugs, perhaps slightly contributed to by the fact that he developed a very strong positive transference to his psychotherapist. He became cheerful, talkative, though the talk showed 'little increase in real insight'. He had several evenings out with his wife, at business dinners, a thing he has not done for some years, and acquitted himself creditably in his own eyes. He also resumed sexual relations with his wife after a gap of about two years, and seemingly with some enjoyment. Shortly before discharge he had two weeks in Sweden with his family. He was discharged as 'symptomatically improved', still on librium. Followed up a week later. Coping fairly well, although he complained of tiredness and gastric pains. His neurosis has always tended towards bowel symptoms. Reassurance was given.

His wife gave this account of him at an interview with the doctor:

'For about fourteen years he has been gradually developing along the lines of which his suicidal attempt is the culmination. He has had various complaints during this time, and has gone from doctor to doctor at intervals without satisfaction. Whenever anything has happened to him, it's always in the worst possible way. If he has a headache, it is a terrible one. The birth of our son was the most difficult in the hospital. He has never been able to accept responsibility for the minor accidents of life. If he drops a cup, it is always somebody else's fault, someone must always be blamed for things, never himself—even things which aren't blameworthy anyway.'

A summary of the case read: this is a case of a severe, chronic neurosis at the very least. He was at one time considered to be psychotic, i.e. an involutional depression with paranoid features. He has a long history of great personal and social difficulties. His physical health is very poor. He has contracted a major physical illness, and he has had a number of more minor ones. On the positive side, he seems to have a reasonably stable marriage and to have raised one child successfully. One would think, however, that on the whole the prognosis is poor. In the hospital the major treatment seems to have been physical, but in a setting of intensive community therapy, and a strong transference to the doctor has been described.

At the first follow-up after leaving hospital: 'He seems to be coping, but only just. He has difficulty entertaining his business friends and in fact says he dreads it. He is still very preoccupied with various physical symptoms and his nerves. It is an effort for him to go out. He says he is hardly any better and relies on regular supplies of drugs to keep going. He sees a psychotherapist for consultations periodically and derives some assurance from this.' At the second follow-up four years later: 'He reported that he had been seeing the same analyst regularly once a month or so since leaving the therapeutic community "just to talk". Takes librium and tofranil three times a day. He feels, however, that he will be able to cut this down eventually. He has had trouble with his shoulder—a bone pressing on the nerves—and he must wear a collar for this. He has also had some kidney trouble. The ulcer discovered during treatment is now much better and needs no treatment for it. His TB is also stabilized.'

As far as the therapeutic community is concerned such a case is clearly a 'failure'.

Mrs L., aged 35

Was admitted to the therapeutic community at Claybury complaining of anxiety symptoms. Initially these have presented as a fear of ill health, and were probably related to the fact that her mother was neurasthenic and was very much frightened about her health for most of her life. She was also worried because her brother-in-law had a heart condition. It was felt, however, that these fears of physical illness were only a screen to her anxiety about her own immaturity and her anxiety about playing an adult female role in life, highlighted, perhaps, by an intense dread of childbirth. She was frightened about going out and frightened that she might fall, and these seem clearly to be fears of a sudden regression back to a state of infantile dependence. Initially the unit staff were extremely pessimistic about her prognosis, since for some months after admission she remained completely preoccupied with her physical symptoms and her phobias, and maintained a very rigid, defensive attitude, resisting any attempts to probe for underlying causes. After some eight months in the unit she started to make progress. She managed to ventilate a good deal of hostility about her marriage, which apparently had been on the point of breaking up. She felt that her husband was a weak, dependent man, and there seems to have been considerable competition as to who could avoid the most responsibility.

On discharge she was thought to be much improved, that she had gained a great deal of insight, and that she was able to work out her problems in a more realistic way, including tackling her husband more directly.

She failed to respond to the year follow-up, but came some forty miles to hospital (accompanied by her husband) for the five-year follow-up interview. She had had no further psychiatric treatment, and she felt that she was dealing quite adequately with her responsibilities in her home. Although she still had panic attacks, these had lessened in intensity and she was able to cope better with them. She refused to take drugs. Her husband confirmed her improvement. They both felt that their marital relations had never been better. It was felt that although she still had obvious neurotic difficulties there was a considerable increase in her ability to handle them, and that both she and her husband had achieved more satisfactory relations.

CHAPTER 7

Research in psychotherapy

Psychotherapeutic systems, as we have attempted to show, are based on (usually tacit) value judgments which too often masquerade as scientifically established principles. This does not mean, however, that they do not 'work'; and the first duty of any therapist should be to show in a reasonably objective and, if possible, replicable way how effective his treatment is. This activity has been common enough among therapists, whether in the form of publication of a series of 'typical' case histories, percentage 'success' versus percentage 'failure', or the comparison of treated with untreated cases. It would be very wrong to deny the importance of this kind of activity, and yet, especially when 'outcome' is considered with little or no reference to the context in which treatment is set, it is essential to clarify the limited usefulness of its application. In effect it does little more than provide the therapist with an excuse for continuing his practice—to our knowledge no method of treatment has ever been *dis*continued or abandoned as the result of adverse research findings—the 'dispassionate' scientist is a master of rationalization when he is placed in difficult circumstances by his data!

Quite apart from the extremely complex problem of the measurement of psychotherapeutic improvement (or otherwise) and the obvious value judgments which this involves, how much further on are we when, for example, Wolpe (1962) claims a 90 per cent (or more) recovery or improvement rate in patients treated by behaviour therapy (although, apparently, this claim has subsequently become rather more modest—Wolpe, Salter and Reyna 1964—reduced, in fact, to 65 per cent)? What do we really learn from Professor Eysenck when he tells us (1952) that patients treated by psychotherapy get no better than patients not treated at all? What good is it to us to read a typical psychiatric or psychoanalytic account of a successfully treated case? The answer depends on how satisfied we are with the concepts of 'psychotherapy' or 'no treatment', 'patients' or 'therapists'. These are generalities, sounding like recognizable entities. However, they are quite empty of meaning. Only those who have succumbed to a completely mechanistic view of a psychological science which treats its subject matter (i.e. people) as almost totally inert and passive, reactive only to the push and pull of the crudest, most general, and most obviously (if loosely) specifiable 'variables' will feel much enthusiasm for this kind of approach. Thus it is essential to recognize that the majority of 'outcome' studies of this kind, which give only cursory consideration to the variables involved in the treatment situation, show only (sometimes) *what* has happened to the patient under consideration, not *how* it happened, nor how *effective* the treatment has been, nor, above all, how *valid* the particular theory behind the treatment may be.

Kiesler (1966) has pointed out some of the myths which underlie this crude kind of approach to research into the outcome of treatment—the myth, for example, that all patients within a broad diagnostic category are all the same and will be affected similarly by the therapeutic process. One might elaborate this to include the myth, or at least the assumption, that patients who find themselves in similar objective circumstances, or whose childhoods show common features, are likely to react to these circumstances in similar ways. This appears to be the assumption behind many papers describing single cases, which go to great lengths to specify the apparently 'causative' features in the patient's background; presumably the publication of such material is frequently felt to be justified by the belief that one will be able to predict what will happen when another patient, with a similar background, appears on the scene. This approach (as pointed out in chapter 2) all too often overlooks the patient's *subjective* view of his circumstances. Kiesler goes on to discuss the further myth that all therapists, whether 'psychotherapists' in general or 'psychoanalysts' in particular, will be the same, that is, more similar than they are different. He also attacks the myth of 'spontaneous remission'—the idea that neurotic patients improve or recover in time with no treatment at all. His argument in this respect is largely based on Rosenzweig's (1954) reply to Eysenck's arguments and on other largely technical questions which need not concern us here, but beyond this, one may make a more general point of some interest. The spontaneous remission argument assumes one of two things: either that *(a)* 'no treatment' is equivalent to a psychological vacuum (this is implied by the adjective 'spontaneous', which appears to discount the fact that remission may be due to therapeutic events outside formal treatment—this point is made by Bergin, 1966), or that *(b)* one can consider as psychotherapeutic only a formalized treatment programme carried out in a medical or quasi-medical situation. Since argument *(a)* appears to involve a patent absurdity, one must assume that 'spontaneous remission' implies argument *(b)*. If all that is required is to show that (considering 'psychotherapy' as a broad, specifiable and concrete mechanical process, and assuming that all patients are more alike than different, likewise all therapists) 'psychotherapy' is no more effective than 'no psychotherapy', then one may be forced to conclude that it is useless. If, however, one wishes to argue that psychiatric symptoms or psychological disturbance cannot be successfully ameliorated by interpersonal psychological methods, one will need very much better evidence than this. In other words, only knowing *that* patients improve or do not improve does not tell us *why* they do or do not improve, nor does it tell us anything about the nature of psychotherapy. Eysenck's arguments are effective only against the person who believes that 'neurosis' and 'psychotherapy' are two homogeneous, well-defined and mechanical processes, which vary in no way from person to person or situation to situation. The layman, seduced into the belief that 'modern science' has reduced the whole problem to one of blinding clarity, could be forgiven for succumbing to such persuasion. The professional, acutely aware of the complexity of the issues involved, could not. We have already mentioned in an earlier chapter Bergin's (1966) documentation of the fact that some psychotherapists can improve patients beyond a level achieved by control subjects, others can make them worse. He concludes that 'Consistently replicated, this is a direct and unambiguous refutation of the oft-cited Eysenckian position.'

However, even if one could consider the Eysenckian position successfully refuted by such an argument, we are still little better off; and the psychotherapist would certainly not be justified in using this as an excuse to sit back happily and carry on as before—after all, he may be one of those who are consistently damaging his patients, and even were he assured of one hundred per cent success, he would still not know the reasons for it. The greatest error of all is to assume that a successful outcome to treatment justifies the theoretical beliefs of the therapist, and, where committed, reflects the thoughtlessly empirical outlook so often met with in psychiatric treatment. So many variables operate within even the simplest and most austere therapeutic situation that the therapist can never be sure that the aspects of the treatment which he believes to be effective really have any influence at all on the situation; and it is perfectly possible that other variables, which he believes to be irrelevant or which he even tries to eradicate (for example, by being 'neutral'), are in fact playing a major role in the recovery or non-recovery of his patient.

With these difficulties in mind, American research workers have by and large turned away from purely 'outcome' problems in psychotherapy research, and have addressed themselves to the even more exacting task of unravelling 'process' variables. The two approaches are not, of course, mutually exclusive: it is more a matter of emphasis either on what therapy achieves or on how it achieves it.

About fifteen years ago Gilbert (1952) wrote: 'One of the extremely important problems in psychological counselling and therapy is that concerning the need for being able to describe and quantify different types of psychotherapeutic relationships. The possibility of accomplishing this is basic to further studies concerning the relative effectiveness of different types of counselling procedures. Studies of this nature will be necessary before it will ever be possible to make any scientific statements regarding such basic questions as the relative effectiveness of different counselling procedures with different types of counselee problems, or the relative effectiveness of a single overall approach to all types of counselling problems as compared with diverse approaches based upon various diagnostic categories.'

The degree of complexity in the psychotherapeutic situation which American workers felt able to tackle ten years ago is impressive (see, for example, Rubinstein and Parloff 1959). The general attitude of many of these workers is well summed up by Sundberg and Tyler (1963), who argue that questions on whether or not psychotherapy 'does any good' are in that form unanswerable, and that research designs should be aimed at dealing with the more limited questions of what kinds of therapeutic technique, what kinds of therapist, and what kinds of treatment conditions have the most beneficial effects on specific kinds of patients.

In the last decade or so, a great deal of light has been thrown on the variables operative in psychotherapy; and while perhaps few, if any, clear-cut principles can be said to have been firmly established, it is high time that some at least of the indications arrived at in this research were seriously considered by the practitioners of psychotherapy. In this country at least, few proponents of the established schools of psychological treatment seem to be prepared to listen to anything but the confirmation and elaboration of their own beliefs and prejudices.

It is the primary purpose of this chapter to draw attention to the findings of research into the processes involved in psychotherapy, particularly those findings which show signs of becoming reasonably well established. These findings have much to do with the nature of the relationship between therapist and patient, and with the effects that the personality of the therapist may have on this. This discussion is thus of the greatest relevance to the general argument and orientation of this book.

Strupp (1962) points out that, in examining the effectiveness of psychotherapy, psychologists began to realize that 'it is pointless to compare percentage figures in the absence of precise information of what is being compared'. He delineates four broad classes of variables to which attention must be paid if an adequate understanding of the psychotherapeutic process is to be attained. These are (1) patient variables, (2) therapist variables, (3) psychotherapeutic method (or technique) variables, and (4) variables operative outside the formal therapeutic situation such as interpersonal relations, environmental circumstances, and so on. These, however, cannot be seen as watertight compartments which one can examine independently of each other, and the fact that complex interactions between patient, therapist and environment must also be investigated is enough to daunt even the most confident research worker.

For the purposes of this discussion we shall begin by considering a selection of those studies in the literature which deal with questions of therapeutic technique. Many 'outcome' studies have dealt with 'psychotherapy' with comparatively little consideration for the theoretical position of the therapists, let alone their personalities. There is little doubt that gross differences exist in the theoretical beliefs of a Freudian compared, say, to a Jungian or a Rogerian psychotherapist. But how do such beliefs *really* affect the type of relationship established between therapist and patient, and influence what *actually* happens between them?

A series of studies by Fiedler (1950*a*, 1950*b*, 1951) appears to demonstrate that therapists of various schools—psychoanalytic, Adlerian and Rogerian—are alike more than they are different, in that ultimately they place more emphasis on the quality of the therapeutic relationship than on the application of technique. Experienced therapists, in particular, are rated as more similar to each other when compared *across* schools than are experienced and inexperienced therapists within the *same* school. Fiedler concludes that the expert brings an empathic understanding to bear on his patient rather than an intellectual one, and, despite the emphasis placed upon it by orthodox psychoanalysts, 'emotional distance' does not appear to play an essential role. This may, of course, be true for a number of experienced psychotherapists (defined by Fiedler as a therapist known nationally as a leading exponent of his school), but it would not be safe to generalize such findings to all psychotherapists, even excluding the inexperienced. Fiedler's first paper (1950*a*) is especially open to criticism, since it relied on what therapists *say* they believe on the basis of questionnaire (Q-sort) items, many of which seemed heavily loaded in respect of the type of answer they were likely to draw. Thus his conclusion that therapists of the different schools already mentioned characterize the ideal therapeutic relationship as one of warmth, empathy and understanding has to be balanced against the degree to which one would expect them to rate favourably the idea that the therapist should 'flounder around' or 'shower his patient with sympathy'. Only the most naïve therapist, surely, would feel tempted to approve behaviour so obviously disapproved of by the designer of the study. Some therapists, moreover, outside the setting of Fiedler's studies, quite specifically condone and recommend the therapist's maintenance of 'emotional distance' from the patient. Macalpine (1950), in a paper purporting to elucidate the nature of the 'transference' relationship in the traditional psychoanalytic situation, sees as one of the analyst's primary aims the *frustration* of the patient's desire for a psychologically close relationship with him. She quotes Freud's view that 'it is expedient to deny [the patient] precisely those satisfactions which he desires most intensely and expresses most importunately', and goes on to characterize the patient's position, in psychoanalysis, as one in which 'He [the patient] gives confidence and gets none in return. . . . He expects analysis to become a partnership, but he is left alone.' The transference, in Macalpine's view, is a one-way relationship in which the analyst, if the patient is to 'regress' satisfactorily, must remain aloof: 'The analysand—uninitiated in the technique—will not only expect answers to his questions, but he will expect conversation, help, encouragement and criticism.' It is clear, however, that as far as this technique is concerned, his expectations will not be met. And the emphasis, most definitely, is on *technique*.

Strupp (1958*a*) compared the reactions of fourteen Rogerian psychotherapists (who were psychologists) and sixty-four psychoanalytically oriented psychotherapists (also psychologists) to a filmed interview conducted with a neurotic patient by an inexperienced psychiatric resident. Both the Rogerian and the psychoanalytic therapists were relatively experienced groups. At various points during the filmed interview the therapists were invited to indicate what they would do at that particular juncture.

Rogerians gave more favourable prognoses to the patient, and had a generally more positive attitude towards him. They were less inclined than the analysts to discourage behaviour of which they disapproved, and less inclined to set up therapeutic goals for the patient. The Rogerian emphasis was on providing a 'corrective emotional experience' by conveying respect for the patient and clarifying feelings. The analytic emphasis (though one suspects that this was not psychoanalysis in 'pure culture') was on interpretation, reassurance and firmness, in which the therapist uses his role to induce change. Rogerians found the approach of the film psychiatrist inadequate, while the analysts found it adequate (Strupp, in fact, characterizes him as definitely inadequate). The analysts (contrary to what we might expect on theoretical grounds) were more ready to give direct answers to the patient from time to time than were the Rogerians, who persevered with 'reflection of feeling'. In the discussion section of this paper, Strupp suggests that a positive attitude on the part of the therapist may be conducive to a positive outcome to therapy, and that the converse may also be true. Over the total sample, there was a significant correlation (0·39) between the therapists' self-ratings of positive conscious attitude towards the patient and favourable prognosis.

In a further paper, using the same experimental situation, Strupp (1958*b*) compared the reactions of fifty-five psychiatrists and fifty-five psychologists, matched for length of experience and personal analysis. Here there were few marked differences between the groups. The aims of the psychiatrists were a little more modest than those of the psychologists—the former stressed symptom relief, the latter the goal of greater insight. The psychiatrists were generally rather more authoritarian and disciplinarian, and advocated less intensive forms of psychotherapy than the psychologists. The psychologists tended to favour the Rogerian approach to therapy rather more; but there were no differences in warmth or coldness of emotional tone between the two groups. Again Strupp notes the tendency for a less empathic (colder) approach to correlate with unfavourable prognosis.

Strupp's views on therapeutic technique frequently seem somewhat equivocal. On several occasions he takes the position (1960,

1962) that the therapist's personal characteristics, though important, are not enough, and that technique is of the greatest significance. He cites (1960) the views of Macalpine, which we have outlined above, with apparent approval, yet he goes on to maintain that certain qualities of the analyst (for example, integrity, dedication and honesty) are 'central to psychoanalysis as a technique'. Thus the very term 'technique' begins to shade into personal characteristics not easily conceived of as technical acquisitions—as Strupp himself says: 'The person of the therapist and his technique are inextricably interwoven.'

Grossman (1952) carried out a study to examine the degree to which insight increased in 'patients' (actually students interested in psychotherapy) following recognition by the therapist of their own explicit feelings as compared with interpretations based on their implicit, unrecognized feelings. Two groups of ten subjects each were employed. Both groups felt, subjectively, equally accepted by the therapist, equally non-dominated by him, and equally understood. The 'deep' (implicit) group rated the sessions (three of one hour each) as having been of more benefit to them, and the therapist rated them more favourably. This group also developed a greater degree of insight over time than did the 'surface' (explicit) group—one measure of insight was the degree to which subjects' judgments of how they scored on a personality inventory agreed with how they actually did score. Grossman feels, however, that despite the care taken in matching the two groups, the 'deep' group were on average more favourable to the idea of psychotherapy, and more expectant of success—attitudes which may clearly account for the results just as well as the level of interpretation or therapeutic intervention.

Dittman (1952) reports a study of a single therapist–patient pair in which were examined the effects of three variables of therapeutic technique—the participation, or attentiveness, of the therapist; his concentration on interpersonal behaviour as compared to feeling states of the patient; and the level (depth) at which his comments were aimed. Ratings were made of these variables from recorded therapy sessions, and also of the degree of therapeutic 'movement' (towards or away from improvement) made by the patient immediately following therapist responses characterized in one these three ways. Dittman summarizes his results as follows: 'Progressive therapeutic movement was found to be associated with (*a*) high level of participation on the part of the therapist; *and* (*b*) response to either feeling or interpersonal behaviour or both. . . . Progressive therapeutic movement was also found to be associated with therapist responses which were slightly deeper than pure "reflection".'

The difficulty with many such studies is in deciding how far the results may be relevant to psychotherapeutic relationships in general, and again how far the often rather artificial setting, necessitated by the experimental design of some of the work described, accurately reflects the real therapeutic situation. Nevertheless, any information on this complex problem is welcome; and one might hope that, through the collection of an increasing number of studies, eventually a coherent and consistent picture of some of the major variables in psychotherapeutic technique may begin to emerge—in fact, we shall be returning to this question later in this chapter.

It was pointed out in the last chapter that some patients seemed, on the basis of test scores and also in terms of diagnosis, to be more suitable than others for treatment in the therapeutic community neurosis unit. The problem of what makes a 'suitable patient' for psychotherapy has been tackled by several workers. For instance, Cartwright and Lerner (1963), using scores derived from Kelly's repertory grid technique, showed that 'need to change' was positively related to Rogerian therapists' ratings of improvement in patients. Strupp (1962) summarizes some of the findings in this field of inquiry as follows: 'A number of studies (Rubinstein and Lorr 1956, Lorr, Katz and Rubinstein 1958, Frank *et al.* 1957, Imber *et al.* 1956) have presented converging evidence on those characteristics of patients which, actuarially, make them good candidates for psychotherapy. These people tend to be well educated, articulate and socially responsible; they are members of the middle class, have a considerable measure of "ego strength", are not deriving excessive secondary gains from their neurotic difficulties via incapacitating somatic illnesses, are anxious, and are eager to do something about their problems. This does not mean, except in a superficial sense, that they are "well" or "normal". In fact, these people often are chronically disturbed in their interpersonal relations and extremely unhappy in their personal and professional lives.' Strupp also quotes Sullivan, Miller and Smelser (1958), who concluded from their own findings that 'Those persons who are least equipped to meet life challenges are the ones who stand to gain least from psychotherapy.'

It is probably too early to conclude from these studies, and others like them, that the patients who most need psychotherapeutic help are incapable of deriving any benefit from it. This may, of course, be a hard fact of life which in the end the profession will be forced to accept, but, on the other hand, it may only apply in the forms of psychotherapy most widely in vogue at the present time—most psychotherapeutic theories do, after all, lay a good deal of emphasis on the stressful nature of therapy and on the degree to which the patient must contribute out of his own resources to his recovery. There are, however, those who believe (e.g. Searles 1965) that, with suitable technical modifications, even schizophrenics—surely the most 'damaged' of all psychiatric patients—can benefit from psychotherapy. It would seem wiser from every point of view, ethically as well as scientifically, to seek ways of adapting psychotherapeutic 'technique' to the needs of patients, rather than excluding from treatment those patients known to be unlikely to respond to a therapeutic model conceived of as immutable. One might envisage, or at least hope for, a situation where there may be several 'kinds' of psychotherapy, each suited to rather different 'kinds' of patients. It will take many more years of research before it can be decided whether or not this is possible, and in what way, and for whom, such therapeutic variations may be achieved. What we do know is that, as things stand, some patients tend to do better than others in psychotherapy, and therapists, in their everyday clinical work, should become aware of and apply rational selection procedures based on the relevant research results so far. For the individual therapist, this means in effect that he should establish which kinds of patients he is able to treat with reasonable success, rather than assume that he has a blanket treatment to cover the whole field of, say, neurosis.

We have already demonstrated (chapter 4) that psychiatric in-patients tend to adopt attitudes towards their illness and its treatment similar to those advocated by, in particular, the medical staff in the institution in which they are treated. We have not so far been able to determine the significance of this in terms of the degree to which patients improve or do not improve—in other words, we do not know whether a patient who adopts the approved attitudes improves more than a patient who resists them. However, there is some evidence that, in related spheres at least, this may be so. This work centres in particular on the field of moral values. For example, Rosenthal (1955) examined attitudes towards sex, aggression and discipline in twelve non-psychotic patients and their therapists, as well as their scores on the Allport–Vernon Study of Values questionnaire. Patients who were rated as most improved also showed moral views most changed in the direction of those of their therapists, while patients who were least improved moved further away from their therapists in this respect. Therapist–patient scores on the Allport–Vernon test showed no consistent relationship, nor indeed had the author expected any, since he did not consider that the kinds of values tapped by his test (e.g. political, religious, aesthetic, economic, etc.) were relevant to the therapeutic situation. What is not clear from this study, however, is how *variable* the therapists' moral views were—were the patients responding to the moral outlook of a single individual, or to a generalized therapeutic ethic common to all therapists? An examination of the questions involved suggests that the latter alternative may have been the case—it is hard to imagine (which would be necessary had there been any real heterogeneity among the therapists in this sample) a therapist who holds that sex is evil and unhealthy, aggression wicked rather than to be accepted and in some degree necessary, and so on.

A questionnaire tapping thirteen different 'Ways to Live' has been developed by Morris (1956) and applied to normals and to psychiatric patients (Morris *et al.* 1960) to establish their conceptions of 'the good life'. These authors found that in general patients' values are very similar to those of normals, and suggest that psychotherapy should be directed at opening the way for patients to achieve their goals in life rather than at changing their values. Many people may react with suspicion, even distaste, to this rather naïvely pragmatic approach to the problem of measurement of 'the good life', but that issue is beside the point in the present context. Also beside the point is consideration of what therapists should do —our interest is at present focused more on what actually happens in therapy.

A study by Welkowitz, Cohen and Ortmeyer (1967) makes use of the Ways to Live scale in a manner rather more relevant to our present inquiry, and also provides an indirect answer to the question concerning homogeneity of therapists' values raised in the Rosenthal study already described. In fact, these workers found that therapists' values (on the Ways to Live scale as well as the Strong Vocational Interest Blank) were as heterogeneous as those of their patients—values here are, of course, rather different from the more conventionally moral questions dealt with in Rosenthal's study. Nevertheless, the findings of Welkowitz and her colleagues are very similar to Rosenthal's. Thirty-eight therapists from two psychoanalytic training centres and forty-four of their patients were studied. It was found that therapists and their own patients were closer in values than those randomly paired, and that the patients rated as most improved by their therapists were closer to them in values than patients rated least improved. The authors conclude that 'The proposition that values move toward similarity in ongoing therapist–patient dyads was not refuted.' In addition, they suggest that where a therapist–patient pair has qualitative, as opposed to merely quantitative, differences in value systems—for example, where marked class differences exist—therapy may be terminated by the patient's 'dropping out'.

A rather discordant note is struck by Rapoport's (1960) observation that, in his study of the Social Rehabilitation Unit at Belmont, improved patients tended to be those who had *rejected* the unit's ideology. In view of this, we should perhaps hesitate to assume too readily that patients' adoption of their therapists' moral outlook or value systems is necessarily an indication of therapeutic gain. The effects of differing circumstances and the general therapeutic situation will have to be investigated more thoroughly before such a conclusion becomes possible, and criteria of improvement will have to be established independently of the therapists' judgment.

Studies of 'therapist variables'—that is, the qualities of therapists most important to successful therapeutic outcome—have become increasingly common in the literature, and have by and large produced surprisingly consistent results. A pioneering effort in this field was that by Whitehorn and Betz (1954). The degree of improvement of 100 schizophrenic patients was rated from case notes, and fourteen doctors were divided into a successful (A) and an unsuccessful (B) group on the basis of their record with these patients. Characteristics of these two groups of therapists were studied, again in terms of ratings derived from case notes for which they had been responsible. It was found that 'A' doctors gained the confidence of their patients and approached their problems by attempting to understand the motivation behind them, whereas 'B' therapists tended to use a descriptive/narrative, biographical sort of approach. 'A' doctors also formulated goals for their patients which were couched in terms of personality variables rather than being merely anti-psychopathological—i.e. focused more on insight into personal capabilities and relationships than on mitigation and control of symptoms. There was a greater tendency for the 'A' physicians to participate actively and personally in the therapeutic situation rather than to adopt a 'professional', distant kind of role. Thus the 'A' doctor could take an active part in the relationship, 'honestly disagree' with his patient if he wanted to, and so on. This contrasted with approaches of the 'B' doctor described by the authors as 'passive-permissive', 'interpretation and instruction' and 'practical care only'. It should be emphasized that these findings were for schizophrenic patients only, as the authors established that the improvement rate for these patients did not correlate with that for other diagnostic categories for any given doctor.

A study by Bandura (1956) examined the effects of anxiety on therapeutic competence. Forty-two therapists rated each other on degree of anxiety concerning feelings of dependency, hostility and sexuality, these ratings then being correlated with supervisors' ratings of therapeutic competence. Moderate, significant correlations were obtained, in a negative direction, between the average ratings of anxiety and psychotherapeutic competence. No significant correlations were obtained between *insight into* anxiety (measured by the similarity between the average group rating and the therapist's self-rating) and competence, nor between competence and self-ratings of anxiety. Thus anxiety appears to hinder therapeutic competence, and mere insight into anxiety is not sufficient to improve matters. The difficulty here is that one can never be sure that supervisors' ratings of therapeutic competence constitute a valid measure, since one may be tapping the supervisors' stereotype of what makes a good therapist—that such a stereotype exists is clearly demonstrated by Holt and Luborsky's (1958) study mentioned in chapter 5.

By far the greater part of research into the characteristics of therapists has been carried out in connexion with Carl Rogers' school of client-centred therapy. Rogers has himself in an important policy statement (1957) outlined his beliefs concerning the necessary and sufficient conditions of therapeutic personality change. The necessary conditions for such change he sees as follows:

1. Two persons are in psychological contact.
2. The first (i.e. the client) is in a state of incongruence, being vulnerable or anxious.
3. The second (i.e. the therapist) is congruent or integrated in the relationship.
4. The therapist experiences unconditional positive regard for the patient.
5. The therapist experiences an empathic understanding of the patient's internal frame of reference, and is able to communicate this to the patient.
6. The therapist is able to achieve such communication to a minimal degree.

'Incongruence' refers to a discrepancy between the self as perceived and actual experience (which may be expressed symbolically, for example, in symptomatic form). Therapist congruence and genuineness Rogers considers to be the antithesis of the professional facade, and he stresses that this means the therapist *being* himself, bad as well as good. Positive regard means the therapist's acceptance of the patient and *his* bad sides as well as his good ones—'caring for the client as a *separate* person', without placing any demands upon him: in other words, accepting in preference to approving. Empathy is the penetration and understanding of the other person's world, being able to adopt his point of view. Rogers feels that these principles apply to all forms of psychotherapy, and that one does not need different approaches for different kinds of patients—techniques of therapy, as well as emphasis on diagnosis as a precondition to therapy, he believes, are unimportant as long as the conditions he stresses are met. Moreover, he feels that intellectual training has no place in the acquisition of these qualities: they are the result of experience which 'may be but usually is not' part of a professional training. From this it can be seen that Rogers puts forward a challenging and radical view of the effective ingredients of psychotherapy, which calls into question a great deal of the established doctrine, derived in large part from psychoanalysis, concerning therapeutic technique and the role of the therapist. It is clear, however, if one bears in mind views on the therapeutic relationship discussed earlier in this book, that others have arrived at beliefs not dissimilar from those expressed by Rogers.

The effects of therapists' empathy were examined in the study by Cartwright and Lerner (1963) already mentioned. Here empathy was measured by the accuracy of the therapist's estimation of the way the client used constructs (i.e. descriptive attributes) arrived at in the repertory grid technique to describe himself—in other words, the *patient's* view of himself compared with the *therapist's* view of the patient's view of himself. Empathy was, indeed, found to be related to the therapists' ratings of their clients' improvement, but only when empathy was measured at the end of therapy. In fact, improved cases became *less* like their therapists' estimations of them at the start of therapy, and unimproved cases *more* like their therapists' initial estimations. This implies, agreeing well with Rogerian theory, that for a successful outcome the therapist must, over time, come to understand the patient's 'real self', rather than the patient forcing himself into the mould set for him by the therapist. Here, of course, the picture is confused by the measure of improvement used, since it is not independent of, indeed is solely dependent on, the therapists' own feelings.

By far the most impressive body of research in the Rogerian frame of reference is that carried out largely under the direction of C. B. Truax. Following for the most part Rogers' definitions of them, Truax has developed standard rating scales for the measurement of therapist genuineness or self-congruence (1962*a*), unconditional positive regard (1962*b*), and accurate empathy (1961). In studies too numerous to be mentioned in detail here, Truax and his colleagues have shown these three therapeutic conditions to be consistently related to positive outcome in psychotherapy with different kinds of patients, including neurotics (Truax *et al.* 1966*a*), schizophrenics (Truax 1963) and delinquents (Truax *et al.* 1966*b*) and using a variety of measures of outcome ranging from specific test scores and ratings of global improvement to criteria such as length of time spent outside the treatment institution. Also consistently replicated has been the finding that a low amount of these therapist variables is related to deterioration in the condition of patients over time spent in psychotherapy. Therapist warmth, or 'unconditional positive regard' has not, however, behaved quite as consistently as the other two conditions mentioned, and in one case turned out to be negatively related to them (Truax *et al.* 1966*a*). In a recent communication, Truax and Wargo (1966) review over twenty papers which confirm the findings discussed above in a way that must make even the most determined critic pause for thought. These authors also consider evidence which suggests that the conditions of warmth, empathy and genuineness may exist in the therapist independently of training or expert knowledge, and that they may be communicated and learned in a teaching situation which places emphasis on acquisition through experience rather than through the straightforward, didactic handing down of 'knowledge'; these points, however, cannot yet be considered to have been established with any certainty. Truax and Wargo conclude that 'One implication of these findings suggests that a sizable number of therapists are unable to provide high levels of empathy, warmth and genuineness, and are therefore likely to provide psychotherapeutic encounters that change people for the worse. Such a clear implication from research raises a host of profoundly distressing practical and ethical problems. It suggests that emphasis in professional evaluation has rested too strongly on theoretic knowledge at the expense of personal skill.'

This research in general lends a great deal of empirical weight to views on the nature of the psychotherapeutic relationship expressed not only by Rogers, but also by some of the theorists whose beliefs were discussed in chapter 2 of this book—for example, Jung, Jourard, and the existential analysts, most of whom, one suspects, would assent with few reservations to Truax and Wargo's suggestion that 'These findings might mean that we should aim at being what we *are* in our therapeutic encounters; that we should openly *be* the feelings and attitudes which we are experiencing; most basically, that we should come into a direct personal encounter with the patient, a meeting on a person-to-person basis, which is all too rare.'

Bergin and Solomon (1963) have attempted to take one aspect of this work a step further by relating empathic understanding to various personality factors. Recorded therapeutic interviews of eighteen inexperienced Rogerian therapists were rated on the Truax scale for the amount of accurate empathy displayed; and these ratings were correlated with a number of psychological test scores, notably the Minnesota Multiphasic Personality Inventory (MMPI), and other rating scales (supervisors' ratings of therapeutic competence and ratings of anxiety). The principal findings were that empathy correlated negatively with the MMPI depression and psychasthenia scales, which the authors interpret as indicative of 'subjective discomfort', and positively with supervisors' ratings of therapeutic competence. The 'Intraception' scale of the Edwards Personal Preference Schedule (Edwards 1959), which measures interest shown in analysing one's own and other people's motives, was also negatively related to empathy, contrary to the authors' prediction. They account for this by suggesting that a cognitive/intellectual, interpretative approach on the part of the therapist is in many ways a hindrance to empathic understanding. Both 'Dominance' on the Edwards scale and age of the therapist were positively related to empathy, suggesting, in Bergin and Solomon's view, that assurance and freedom in interpersonal relations help in the formation of the empathic attitude. Supervisors' ratings of competence were, as already mentioned, positively related to empathy and negatively related to ratings of anxiety, but anxiety and empathy showed no significant correlation. This finding both supports and calls into question the results of Bandura's research which was discussed above: Bandura found the same correlation between anxiety and supervisors' ratings, but his conclusion that the latter reflect actual 'in-therapy' behaviour is not supported by Bergin and Solomon in so far as empathy may be considered a measure of this.

The sheer weight of the research evidence concerning warmth, empathy and congruence (or genuineness), drawn from many different patient samples and measured by a wide variety of methods, makes it difficult to draw anything but the obvious conclusions, and almost impossible not to agree with the theorists who hold that 'technique' in psychotherapy, in the traditional sense that it has been applied, is either irrelevant or positively harmful. And yet there is still at least one objection that can be made, and that is that nearly all the studies which have been described above have been carried out in the Rogerian therapeutic orientation. The psychoanalyst might point out that where the therapist does little more than 'reflect the feelings' of his patients and encourage them in this way to follow the therapeutic path of their own choosing, such factors as warmth, empathy and genuineness may indeed be of prime importance, since there is little else in the situation to effect change. In the Freudian situation, on the other hand, a very definite technical process is applied by the therapist, and the patient is *analysed* by means of the regressive transference situation, and psychic processes and mechanisms are activated and interpreted independently of the analyst's personality characteristics—in other words, something is *going on* in the analytic situation which renders such considerations as those thought to be so important by the Rogerians less relevant and essential. A study by Strupp, Wallach and Wogan (1964) goes some way towards meeting this kind of objection, and suggests that the findings of Truax and his co-workers are not relevant only to the Rogerian therapeutic situation.

Strupp and his colleagues administered a complex and thorough, retrospective questionnaire to forty-four psychoneurotic patients (and their therapists) who had had long-term psychotherapy (average two years and four months), for the most part in a psychoanalytic setting. As far as outcome was concerned, only 9 per cent said they were symptom free (nearly three years later) although 74 per cent had at least 'considerably improved' symptomatically. Seventy-one per cent reported a greater awareness of feelings and impulses, greater insight, more enjoyment in life, and so on. Other changes showed in increased self-esteem and better interpersonal relations. Forty-one per cent felt they definitely needed more therapy. Most interesting as far as the present discussion is concerned, however, were the comments made by patients about their experience of the therapist–patient relationships. Patients claiming to have improved rated their therapist's attitude, in retrospect, as warmer, more respectful, natural and unstudied, more attentive, less distant and uncertain. An emphasis on technique and the use of jargon, the interpretation of silences, gestures and bodily posture seemed to these patients anti-therapeutic, and 'intensive' psychoanalytic treatment making use of these techniques did no better, according to patient and therapist ratings, than other forms of therapy. Patients were more impressed by the personality characteristics of their therapists, as far as therapeutic effect was concerned, than by technical interventions. Thus Strupp, Wallach and Wogan conclude that, judging by the patients' subjective evaluation of therapeutic benefit, the personal qualities of the therapist play a central role in the treatment process. The more intensive and psychoanalytic (in the technical sense) the treatment, the poorer, and hence less therapeutic, is the relationship between therapist and patient.

Taken together, these studies present a challenge both to those who maintain that psychotherapy is ineffective as a method of treatment for mental illness, and to those who continue to practice psychotherapy or psychoanalysis as a technical exercise without regard for the basic features of the human relations involved and the central and essential role these appear to play in therapeutic outcome. A great deal of the mystery attached to the psychotherapeutic process seems to be evaporating with the emphasis being placed less on the (theoretical) functioning of complex psychic machinery in the individual patient, and more on the interaction between therapist and patient in respect of more obvious variables, long suspected to be significant on the grounds of common sense alone. The therapist who insists on clinging to a therapeutic technique based largely on purely theoretical beliefs, especially if he denies the importance of his own personal (as opposed to professional) characteristics in the therapeutic process, now has an obligation to demonstrate the validity of his position. Therapeutic 'neutrality', in the sense of a deliberate attempt (which must, one way or another, be in any case doomed to failure) to stay *as a person* outside the therapeutic situation, can no longer be justified.

CHAPTER 8

Implications for psychology and psychotherapy

The ultimate aim of the scientist has often been thought of as the attainment of watertight arguments on the basis of incontrovertible experimental evidence. The merits of competing hypotheses are ideally decided by the 'crucial experiment', where all variables other than those to be manipulated in the experimental conditions are carefully and accurately controlled.

Laudable though such an aim may be, it is unlikely that it is a realistic one as far as the social sciences are concerned. Scriven (1964) has pointed out that, as compared with the physical (natural) sciences, psychology is in an especially difficult position. To begin with, human beings have already 'discovered' most of the more easily established and interesting facts about themselves, if only from their own experience, and the field left for elucidation is extremely complex and subtle, affected by the interplay of an infinite number of variables. Furthermore, man's consciousness introduces a factor which presents a unique complication to the psychological scientist, for, being conscious, a man can deliberately refute almost any prediction made about him. Scriven likens the situation of the psychologist to that of a physicist whose aim is to determine the exact landing-point of a falling leaf. The oft-stated aim of psychology—to arrive at the 'prediction and control' of behaviour—may therefore be in any real sense unattainable. As Scriven suggests, we are dealing with 'the epistemology of incomplete information'.

Given this state of affairs, it is not difficult for any psychologist or psychiatrist with a vested interest in maintaining the *status quo* to erect an impervious barrier against new research findings by the hasty adoption of a tough-minded scientific attitude. All research in the social sciences is easily criticized, for the variables can never all be completely controlled; there is, in practice, hardly ever a perfectly selected sample; the 'crucial experiment' is never quite possible—and all this quite apart from the fact that, as we have pointed out, the theoretical basis, certainly of psychotherapeutic systems, consists largely of assumptions and value judgments which are by their very nature 'unscientific', in that they are not 'objective'.

Thus it is never really difficult to dismiss research findings which conflict with one's preferred practices or beliefs, and this may be why so many fundamentally different theoretical systems can exist side by side in psychology without ever arriving at any real confrontation.

A kind of scientific mythology has grown up in psychology in which a number of methodological slogans have all but taken the place of rational reflection. The effort of behaviouristic psychology to emulate what it took to be the methods of natural science and to found its *raison d'être* in positivism led to generations of psychologists being indoctrinated with technical and experimental considerations of method at the expense of a thoughtful approach to and observation of the data relevant to a psychological science. Thus the emphasis on statistical methodology and experimental design, though undoubtedly beneficial and indeed essential to a properly disciplined science, has become so one-sided that it tends often to be an end rather than a means. Statistical methods these days far outstrip in sophistication the psychological meaningfulness of the data to which they are applied, so that in the end it often appears to be numbers rather than psychological concepts which are being manipulated. No amount of mathematical subtlety can compensate for poor observation and inadequate conceptualization of the psychological phenomena to be considered. In a recent paper, Bakan (1966) has pointed out how psychologists have come to use the statistical 'test of significance' as a method of automatic inference which apparently absolves them from developing the closely reasoned inductive arguments that are the true stuff of scientific thinking. Statistical tests of this kind, in fact, help one with establishing the probabilities associated with the results in the individual experiment under consideration, but they do not establish whether or not the hypothesis underlying the research is true of the wider (non-experimental) population. This should appear self-evident, but all too often the assumption is made that the test lends some kind of ultimate numerical authority to the (tacit) inductive argument from experiment to hypothesis.

In considering sampling techniques, expressions such as 'biased sample' or 'random sample' are too frequently bandied about without consideration of the actual data involved. The ideal random sample is a kind of Platonic 'Form' glibly invoked by the scientific idealist, but in practice is rarely, if ever, attainable. Our own sampling procedures (for example, those used in the research reported in chapter 4) are easily criticized on the grounds that respondents to our questionnaire were all volunteers, and consequently may not represent a broad enough spectrum of opinion. This does, of course, represent a possible bias. And yet what is the alternative? To *force* people to reply to a questionnaire is clearly impossible, and to browbeat unwilling respondents would almost certainly, if successful, result in a bias of another kind. The difficulties in obtaining an adequate sample, as every researcher not in possession of vast funds or without the backing of a large institution knows, are very great, and whatever procedure one might adopt to meet them almost invariably introduces a bias of some kind. The 'tough-minded' scientist might conclude that in this case it is better not to embark on such research at all, as the results will in any case be worthless. The 'tender-minded' scientist, on the other hand, with an interest in reaching some kind of understanding based on reasoned argument rather than solely on a dogmatic belief in faultless methodology, may be prepared to be swayed by considerations such as that (in the case of our own research) the respondents to our questionnaire came from several different hospitals, that it is unlikely that nearly three hundred people are going to show any consistent form of bias, that *in fact* the questionnaire seems to have tapped a broad spectrum of opinion, that the results are in accordance with expectations and show a certain consistency between samples, that other workers have obtained similar findings.

It is not our intention here to erect a blanket defence against criticism, especially of our own work, which clearly has methodological shortcomings, nor do we wish to suggest that there is any excuse for sidestepping problems of research design. We wish only to argue that science advances ultimately by processes of reasoning rather than by rigid adherence to a kind of scientistic dogma which rests on a number of technological articles of faith. Evidence in psychology is never perfect, never watertight, but it should not be dismissed because of this. It can only be replaced by better evidence.

Thus the psychotherapist whose beliefs are jeopardized by the findings concerning the therapeutic relationship discussed in the last chapter cannot simply dismiss them on the basis of technical, statistical, or some other kind of inadequacy, even though he could almost certainly find such inadequacy if he looked for it carefully enough. *Instead he is obliged to search for more convincing evidence to justify his own position.* The scientific attitude is too easily replaced by a kind of querulous scholasticism; and if the critic is waiting for absolute truth to be established before he budges, he will wait for ever, for science proceeds by negation (on the grounds of new evidence) rather than by confirmation.

The greater part of modern research into psychotherapy appears to vindicate the views of those therapists who have emphasized the importance of the immediate nature of the therapeutic relationship, especially as this is affected by the personality of the therapist, and the relative unimportance of any fixed, mechanically conceived technique. The therapist should be able to free himself of theoretical preconceptions to the extent that he can look at the patient's world through the patient's eyes, should be able to accept rather than merely approve of his patients, and should be able to take part in the therapeutic situation as a 'genuine' rather than as a 'professional' person. Thus practice appears to be more important than theory, personality more important than technique.

The fact that some therapists seem to be consistently better than others as far as therapeutic effectiveness is concerned, and that this appears to be related to fairly stable therapist characteristics such as warmth, empathy and genuineness, suggests that, for the patient, it is his immediate experience of therapy and the therapist *as they are* which constitutes the 'corrective emotional experience' rather than the mechanical operation of, for example, regressive transference phenomena. Indeed, as one of us has pointed out elsewhere (Smail 1968), the patient's conscious experience of the therapeutic relationship has been neglected to an astonishing extent by many if not most influential workers in this field, a situation which has led to such concepts as therapeutic 'neutrality'. It seems particularly unrealistic to expect a conscious being to experience one as neutral just because one studiously avoids entering into any kind of directly meaningful relationship with him. The oft-cited psychoanalytic view that the patient 'misunderstands the present in terms of the past' shows an almost arrogant indifference to his present experience, and enables the therapist to play down the importance of his own *personal* involvement in the analytic situation.

Experience of the present must, of course, be influenced in many respects by experience of the past, and the way in which this process comes about need not be conscious. This does not mean, however, that the present is of no significance, or is merely a warped projection of the past.

In fact, the various theoretical languages of psychotherapy and the concepts which they describe might in principle be translatable in terms of each other without any very great difficulty; but it is more the questions of emphasis which are important. Thus one feels that 'unconscious' in psychoanalysis implies something more than the unreflective or habitual application of learned patterns of perception and behaviour, the acquisition of a set of unquestioned assumptions, the development of a personal frame of reference which some other theorists—for example, Kelly (1955), Snygg and Combs (1949), and, on a rather less ambitious scale, Wolf (1966)—have implied. These latter views tend to give to 'unconsciousness' a relatively flexible and individual interpretation, while that of psychoanalysis tends to be relatively rigid and universal, in that both the structure and the content of the unconscious are seen as more rather than less constant, both within and between individuals. Orthodox psychoanalysis, similarly, lays a good deal of emphasis on instinctual (id) mechanisms such as sex and aggression, while more recently derived theories tend to stress learned phenomena and goal-directed behaviour. Thus the issue seems once again to boil down to one of reductionism versus teleology, universality versus individuality.

We have, of course, no grounds besides personal preference for accepting one theory of the causation of mental illness rather than another, even though the less mechanistic orientations seem to receive greater objective justification as far as the way in which they conceptualize the nature of the psychotherapeutic relationship is concerned. The fact that it does not appear helpful to the patient to approach his illness from a mechanical point of view does not mean that his illness was not mechanically derived. And yet the observation that in practice theories of mechanical aetiology are to some degree correlated with a 'distant', technical approach to therapy certainly does suggest that such theories are less (therapeutically) *useful* than those which we have characterized as dynamic and teleological. The postulation of mechanisms enables the theorist to escape the complex problems involved in any consideration of human experience, with its attendant difficulties of subjectivity and individuality. The mechanistic therapist can undercut his patient's experience, especially as this relates to the therapist himself, and replace the individual before him with a model. But this saving in the effort involved in therapeutic understanding is at the patient's expense.

Apart from the fact that this indifference to the phenomena ot experience leads to the therapist's ignoring just those aspects of the therapeutic situation which have been shown to be the most important, it can also produce a kind of unawareness of the significance of experience, which generates puzzling theoretical blind-spots. Salzman (1966) has indicated how psychoanalysis has tended to assume that the child's experience may be understood in terms of the adult's: 'Freud assumed that the infant comprehended the dangers to its existence in adult terms and in adult categories of meaning. The notion of an infantile amnesia required that an infant understand the significance of some of his activities (like masturbation, or other behaviour disapproved of by adults) and repress it because of the fear of rejection or disapproval. It required that the infant deny through an amnesic process some of the forbidden interests and pleasures which the adult presumed he was enjoying.' However, Salzman suggests that 'We have no reason to assume that events transpire in the infant's experience in the same categories of meaning or significance as they do in the adult. It is precisely because none of us can remember what it was like to be an infant that we cannot be sure of the frame of reference of the infant's experiences.' Again: 'It has been assumed that ... repressed feelings, attitudes, percepts or concepts remained encapsulated, timeless and unavailable to the ongoing experience of the individual, and could be recalled into awareness in their original repressed state. This is a highly doubtful conception, since present recall can only take place in the context of the individual's present view of the world as well as his present-day vocabulary and patterns of experiencing.'

Bannister (1966) has argued that one of the cardinal sins of mechanistic psychological theories is that they are not reflexive—that is, the psychologist attempts to account for (to predict and control) the behaviour of everyone but himself. This being outside or above the rules he has postulated for others suggests that the psychologist is either allowing a significance to his experience of himself which he is not willing to give to others, or is merely oblivious to the possibility of there being a problem at all. In any case, he ends up in a paradoxical situation. Bannister's observations on this paradox as it occurs in experimental psychology provide a particularly forceful example of his argument: 'In order to behave like scientists we must construct situations in which our subjects are totally controlled, manipulated and measured. We must cut our subjects down to size. We construct situations in which they can behave as little like human beings as possible, and we do this in order to allow ourselves to make statements about the nature of their humanity. I can think of no simple formula which can allow us to escape from this paradox, but I think we might have the decency to acknowledge its presence. We ought not to use the curious notions of reductionism in order to try to convince ourselves that our chaining of our subjects is the ideal way to go about things. It may be that an imprisoned, minuscule man is all that we are capable of studying, but let us acknowledge that we do miserable experiments because we lack the imagination to do better ones, not claim that these are scientifically ideal because they are simple minded.' Bannister's science fiction characterization of the predicament of the psychologist applies equally well to the psychotherapist: 'The master chemist has finally produced a bubbling green slime in his test-tube, the potential of which is great but the properties of which are mysterious. He sits alone in his laboratory, test-tube in hand, brooding about what to do with the bubbling green slime. Then it slowly dawns on him that the bubbling green slime is sitting alone in the test-tube brooding about what to do with him. This special nightmare of the chemist is the permanent work-a-day world of the psychologist—the bubbling green slime is always wondering what to do about you.' Bannister sees the situation of the psychologist and his subject matter as one of a perpetual race in which each tries to subsume (understand) the behaviour of the other. 'Such an infinite and unending elaboration is perhaps a depressing vista to those who aspire to a deterministic science in pursuit of the holy grail of final truth. It is, however, a comforting thought to those of us who fear unemployment and who like to think that every answer is as good as the question it generates.'

The analogy of the 'bubbling green slime' raises a number of interesting questions about the scientific status of psychological tests as objective measuring instruments or as standard situations in which to observe behaviour. For example, in a series of studies by one of us (Caine 1963, 1966) it was found that when given the opportunity 'normal' subjects tended to suppress the report of socially offensive perceptual stimuli in favour of emotionally innocuous material. Psychotic subjects, on the other hand, tended to report the socially offensive material faithfully when the material presented was directly related to their pathological emotional state. An explanation of these findings was advanced in terms of differences between the two groups of subjects in their interpretations of the test situation as a whole. It was thought reasonable to regard a psychological testing session as essentially a social interaction in which the subject and the tester are the active participants. The testee will respond not only to the test material, but also to the presence of the tester and to his reaction or interpretation of the situation as a whole. (This is admitted, if only implicitly, by even the most rigorously 'scientific' stimulus-response psychologist when he attempts to establish *rapport* with his subjects and get them interested in his research project as such.) That many subjects were vitally concerned with the impression they were making was well indicated in the experimental situation by the number of spontaneous remarks such as, 'Oh, I couldn't say that!' (followed by an innocuous response), or, 'Sorry, doctor, I'm not really like that', etc. One got the strong feeling that what was most important to a subject was not the stimuli being presented, but the need to communicate what sort of a person he was, and that the test material was being selected, edited and reported precisely with this end in view. Perhaps only psychologists need to perform experiments to realize this.

Klein (1958) has advanced a rather similar argument, and considers that what a subject *reports* in any perceptual experiment is always an active process of sifting and choosing among alternatives —a process which always narrows a subject's report of his perception. Even the most rigorously controlled psychophysical experiment in which maximal accuracy is intended is not free from selective report. As an example Klein describes a tachistoscopic experiment in which subjects were being tested for their recognition limens (thresholds) by means of the gradual exposure of a simple line drawing of a triangle. As the time of exposure lengthened, one subject kept repeating that he saw nothing. He gave this report so far beyond the usual limits that the experimenter became suspicious and looked into the tachistoscope himself only to see the triangle quite clearly. He again showed the triangle and asked the subject what he saw, and this time the response came: 'Nothing, only the same old triangle.' Had he been seeing this for some time? 'Yes,' the subject replied. Well, why didn't he say so? 'Well, it didn't seem reasonable to me that you'd have built such a complex, huge apparatus just to show a little old triangle.'

In the field of psychological 'projective' testing Smail (1966) has argued that responses to such tests as the Thematic Apperception Test (TAT) are not automatic. To obtain meaningful results, the stimulus cards presented must be seen by the subject as having some personal relevance to himself and his particular situation. Some evidence was presented, for example, that paranoid patients, traditionally thought to give consistently aggressive responses on the TAT, in fact only appear to do so when the stimulus card enables them to identify themselves with the possible victim of an aggressive act, rather than with the aggressor himself. Psychopaths might well give a similar total number of aggressive responses scored objectively, but their identification would probably be with the aggressor rather than with the victim. As Smail has argued: 'What is claimed is that expectations that apparently similar responses imply similar psychological meaning are very probably unfounded, and to assume this by using a ... global scoring system would be invalid, since the meaning of a response must depend on the context in which it occurs.' A recent attempt to come to terms with this problem and combine the actuarial and clinical approach in diagnostic testing is that of the Symptom-Sign Inventory developed by Foulds (Foulds and Hope 1968), in which the subject is asked a standardized set of diagnostic questions but the psychologist is given some freedom to exercise his clinical judgment in his acceptance of the responses.

It is no doubt true that psychologists today recognize the influence on responses to test stimuli of personality factors, present expectations, need states, value systems, instructional sets and test-taking attitudes. Indeed, such recognition has spread to the most rigidly entrenched areas of intelligence and abilities testing (Eysenck 1967, Foulds and Caine 1958*b*). Dahlstrom (1962), for example, has listed six 'contextual' and five 'mediating' variables which he feels can be invoked to account for the responses obtained to a well-known psychiatric symptom inventory of the questionnaire type. Such variables include the experimental setting, the examiner and the specific test items (contextual variables), as well as the veridical facts, personality styles and test instructions (mediating variables). Some recent evidence suggests that the influence of the more extraneous response determinants is reduced when the test material presented to the subject has direct, personal relevance (Caine and Smail 1967*b*).

There is perhaps no need to labour the point, since our aim in presenting this evidence is merely to suggest that the use of psychological tests as measuring instruments or standardized methods of observation does not automatically make our psychology objective or our statistical manipulations of the scores scientific, since we are seldom certain that our subjects have in fact responded to our narrowly defined experimental stimulus only. The chances are, indeed, that they have not. Psychological testing, in fact, can no more be reduced to a 'standard situation in which to observe behaviour' than can psychotherapy be reduced to a standard method or technique. In this connexion, some psychologists have maintained (e.g. Meehl 1954) that predictions based on standardized test batteries have greater validities than have the judgments of individual clinicians. This is not inevitably so. Kelly and Fiske (1951, p. 159) found that clinically derived assessment ratings and objective test scores were about equal in predictive efficiency, and Holt and Luborsky (1958), and Sawyer (1966) have claimed that some individual clinicians can make better predictions than others, and better, indeed, than predictions based on normative test data. This, of course, provides a similar argument to the 'therapist uniformity myth' expounded by Kiesler (1966) and mentioned in chapter 7. Were it possible to select clinicians for their predictive capacity, their assessments might well obtain higher validities than those based on psychological test scores alone.

We do not wish to suggest, however, that measurement in psychology is an unworthy aim. On the contrary, if we wish to back up our observations concerning people with rational argument, evidence derived from the use of psychological measuring instruments will be essential. But if we are to be able successfully to understand *individuals*, techniques other than those based on the traditional *normative* approach will have to be developed. In more recent years there have been encouraging signs that psychologists are working on this problem. For example, Shapiro (1951) points to the possibility of bringing experimental and statistical techniques to bear on the observation of single patients. Kelly's (1955) repertory grid technique is a particularly good example of one of several correlational techniques which have similarly been applied to intra-individual psychological problems. The thinking of (in particular existential-phenomenological) theorists has given birth to methods of measuring the interpersonal perceptions involved in, for example, married couples or small family groups (Laing *et al.* 1966, Scott and Ashworth 1965).

These are hopeful signs that psychology is progressing beyond the simplistic conception of its subject matter which has been so evident in much of its theory and methodology.

CHAPTER 9

Conclusions

In this book we have put forward the argument that the basic assumptions and value judgments both of those who give and those who receive treatment for mental illness greatly influence the kind of theoretical posture adopted, as well as the outcome of treatment. We have drawn on evidence from several quarters, both our own and other people's, and have related this to some of the most fundamental situations met with by professionals in this field, focusing in particular on the therapeutic relationship.

The individual's past experience, and the assumptions he has developed at least in part as a function of it, colour his whole attitude to the world around him; and this applies as much to the scientist as he formulates his view of science as to anyone else. In science—at least as it is exemplified in psychiatry and psychology, and almost certainly also more generally—assumptions and value judgments contained within its methods and its premisses have become largely disreputable, and hence tacit. To understand the psychiatrist's and the psychologist's scientific philosophy and methods of approach, it is necessary to make them explicit; and to allow those who may need psychological treatment to make a rational choice between one kind of treatment and another, it is necessary for them also to understand the assumptions which underly the 'scientific' procedures put forward by the experts as means of curing or alleviating their suffering.

The social sciences, feeling scientifically inferior, have struggled to earn for themselves reputability in the eyes of their revered forerunners, the natural sciences. With this end in view they have assumed a rigorous objectivism supported by an almost exclusively mechanistic view of man, whether this is couched in medical, statistical or psychoanalytic terms. The result has been that in both the psychotherapeutic and the psychological testing situations the *meaning* of the situation to the participants has largely been neglected.

It has been our aim to draw attention to some of the basic presuppositions brought to these particular situations by the principal protagonists, and to relate these to other psychological phenomena, such as personality characteristics, and also to some extent to the outcome of treatment. This is not to deny that some aspects of behaviour, particularly in the mentally ill, are determined more by the compulsive nature of the patient's psychopathology than by any conscious appraisal of the situation. Nevertheless, it is maintained that present evaluations and conscious awareness may modify behaviour and social interactions even in acute psychosis. To neglect this aspect of human activity can only make our treatments of patients partial and our psychology superficial, mechanical and 'inhuman'.

No doubt this is a common-sense view with which at heart most people would agree. But to *identify* the important elements in such complex interactions as psychotherapy, for example, is a matter of considerable difficulty; and it is our hope that the suggested conceptualizations and measurements put forward in this book have gone some way towards defining some of them.

As far as our own research into the effects of personality and attitudes in the therapeutic situation is concerned, there are clearly many points which remain unanswered and several lines of investigation to be pursued further. There seems to be little doubt that basic attitudes to such questions as what kinds of working relationships should be developed within staff groups, and between patients and staff, may play a large part in deciding what theoretical, and ostensibly scientific, orientation will be adopted by the professional in the field. Moreover, these attitudes do not seem to be directly deducible from a knowledge of the orientation subscribed to; i.e. they are not logically contained within it as a matter of conscious definition. The origin of these attitudes is still not yet clear. They seem to depend at least to some extent on basic components of personality; this has been established particularly well in groups of psychiatrists, as well as in other professional groups such as nurses and occupational therapists. We also have some evidence, not yet fully analysed, that non-professional, 'normal' subjects' attitudes to treatment, as measured by a shortened version of our questionnaire, are related to personality traits very similar to those described for the psychiatrist sample in chapter 5. We have very little evidence, however, on the degree to which attitudes, and indeed possibly even personality, depend upon training procedures; and from this point of view it would clearly be desirable to conduct studies among medical and nursing students, and to follow junior psychiatrists through their early years of training in psychiatric hospitals.

In a rather wider context, those of us who work in mental hospitals are well aware of the interpersonal conflicts aroused by the clash of treatment philosophies. We have in our own experience come across instances of such conflicts between members of staff, and have found that the correlation between their scores on our questionnaire measure of attitudes to treatment approximates zero, whereas for members of staff more able to work harmoniously together, correlations are highly positive. We feel also that the heat generated by such friction may be determined more by the basic personality differences underlying and correlated with the differing treatment philosophies than by differences over technical matters alone. The fact that it seems possible to develop measures, however crude, of these important factors in staff relations and to direct attention to the aspects of personality functioning relevant to the treatment situation, opens up possibilities of bringing rational investigation to a set of problems previously obscured by dogmatic opinion or fatalistically accepted as insoluble.

The fact that individual hospitals may be differentiated in terms of the attitudes of the nurses who work in them and of the patients who are treated in them suggests that the 'institutional atmosphere' may play a large part in the formation of these attitudes, possibly independently of the formal training programmes involved. In this connexion it is interesting to speculate on the position of those individuals whose personality inclines them in a direction away from that of the prevailing institutional influences. After all, it seems unlikely that in their effort to obtain nursing staff, often in the face of acute shortage, administrators of large mental hospitals are going to be influenced very much by an applicant's personality characteristics except as these may be relevant to such obvious factors as honesty, morality and a basic level of intelligence. Thus we would suspect that in these institutions there will be many nurses who, while paying lip-service to the treatment philosophy current in the hospital, will be, because of antipathetic personality traits, basically hostile to it, and consequently their effectiveness as a member of the working community may well be affected. It may be, for example, that the 'traditional' nurse will be more effective, or at least happy, in a 'traditional' hospital than, say, a 'therapeutic community' nurse, with the converse obtaining in a 'therapeutic community' hospital.

Again, although the main argument of this book tends to support the contention that some kinds of treatment are better than others, we should perhaps add: 'for some patients'. It seems safe to say that the effectiveness of treatment depends on a complex interaction between the method of treatment and the presuppositions and personalities of the patient and therapist. It is possible that a patient whose personality and attitudes bias him in favour of, for example, a physical treatment approach, may in fact benefit more from this kind of treatment if it is dispensed by a devotee than by a psychiatrist of a different persuasion. Many psychiatrists, of varied orientations, feel that *faith* in the treatment, on the part of the doctor as well as the patient, is probably essential for success. There would seem to be some scope for the systematic investigation of this hypothesis.

Following on from these considerations, it seems likely that patients treated with drugs in hospital will, because of their doctor's faith in them as effective remedies, learn to use them in emotional crises, and will continue to do so on discharge. In other words, they will come to look upon their own emotional reactions as symptoms of a physically determined illness, and will treat them accordingly. Alternatively, patients treated by psychotherapy will, in similar situations, learn to look for and attempt to come to terms with 'underlying problems' of a basically psychological nature. On following up such patients after discharge, one might well regard the group treated by psychotherapy as the more 'successful' if criteria of improvement included such indices as the continued use of drugs, or visits paid to medical practitioners in order to obtain further supplies of drugs. However, differences in 'successful outcome', characterized in this way, between two such groups would in fact be predetermined by differences in the treatment philosophies involved: they would reflect differences in how the patients had been *taught to handle their emotional crises* rather than any true differences in their state of mental health.

However, all these questions are at this stage purely speculative, and further research is needed before the factors involved can be fully understood.

One thing seems certain: no amount of scientific wishful thinking can obscure the importance of personality and attitudinal factors in the psychotherapeutic relationship except at the cost of grave damage to our understanding of the processes operative in treatment, and ultimately to the patient's chances of recovery or relief from psychological distress. Any future research project designed to evaluate the outcome of treatment or to elucidate the processes involved in treatment (including physical treatments) must, then, take into account such variables as the doctor's personality *in relation to* his conscious treatment orientation and attitudes, and the way in which these are perceived and experienced by his patients. In this respect the doctor's faith in, and enthusiasm for, his treatment may well be defined by the extent of the congruence between the relevant personality traits and his learned treatment attitudes. The extent to which this faith and enthusiasm is accepted sympathetically by the patient may well be determined by the degree of similarity between his own personality and expectations and those of his doctor.

The important personality variables to be considered would be such attributes as 'tough-' and 'tender-mindedness', introverted versus extraverted thinking, sensitivity to emotional states in oneself and in others (some people may prefer to call this 'neuroticism', others, perhaps, 'insight' or 'empathy'), emotional warmth and emotional genuineness. Most studies involving comparative treatment designs—particularly perhaps those using such experimental techniques as the random allocation of patients to psychiatrists of various orientations—have, by overlooking these factors, tended to direct attention away from them.

It may well be necessary to develop instruments specially designed to measure these variables. Our own questionnaire, in particular the first component, has proved useful for measuring attitudes to treatment at the more conscious level. Standardized tests which have shown some promise in distinguishing relevant underlying personality traits include the Cattell 16-PF questionnaire (Cattell and Eber 1957), the Guilford–Martin inventory (used in this connexion by Kreitman 1962), and the Kuder Preference Record (Kuder 1948). Some current work of our own suggests that the Myers–Briggs Type Indicator (Myers 1962) has a distinct contribution to make in measuring what may be a highly relevant 'intuiting' versus 'sensing' dimension (this, in fact, tends to contrast the theoretical, imaginative type with the practical, down-to-earth type; our hypothesis is that people scoring high on the first component of our questionnaire, i.e. the more 'traditional', 'physical treatment' respondents, would tend to fall into the latter group). Other measuring devices which are of interest include Truax's rating scales of warmth, empathy and genuineness (see chapter 7), and Jourard's self-disclosure scales (Jourard 1964).

The influence of such factors as warmth, empathy and genuineness may well be an important consideration in contexts far wider than that of mental health. Industrial psychologists have long been aware of the importance of the quality of the relations between management and the shop floor (see, for example, Jaques 1951). Revans (1964), in a study already referred to, has investigated the effects of staff structure on morale in general hospital nurses; and in the field of physical medicine most people can recount experiences in hospitals, maternity wards, etc., which suggest that the degree of understanding in many of these institutions of the significance of the psychological factors involved leaves a great deal to be desired. Jourard (1964) has gone as far as to suggest that a basic understanding of the psychological needs of the seriously physically ill may make the difference between life and death. The 'taboo against tenderness', the studious avoidance of confrontation with emotional needs and consideration of the individual's experience of his predicament, is an inevitable consequence of the objectivist bias in scientific and quasi-scientific situations, quite apart from wider sociological factors which may contribute to such attitudes (in medicine, for example, one thinks immediately of the rigid, almost military hierarchy of authority and the disciplinarian concepts which this engenders).

It is true that some of these problems, as far as the National Health Service is concerned, are receiving attention at a high level. New hospitals are being built with the patients' personal needs much more in mind than used to be the case; rules for visiting, etc., in children's hospitals have become far less rigid (though not always, and not everywhere); many studies are in progress, often supported by such bodies as the King Edward's Hospital Fund, which are looking into the administrative structure and interpersonal relations involved in hospital staffing. But there are still many treatment situations in which the patient must put up a hard struggle to maintain both his dignity and his identity—one thinks in particular of chronic and geriatric wards in some large mental hospitals.

Much suffering could be alleviated if the administrators and pace-setters in our hospitals recognized and understood the emotional needs of people in physical and mental distress, and if those responsible for treatment acknowledged that assumptions about what science is and what it can study can often result in extensive blind-spots in an otherwise humane approach. As far as psychiatry is concerned, it is our belief also that money spent on research into such factors as those we have mentioned could well pay as great or greater dividends as that spent on research into, say, the physical cause of mental illness. To assume that the 'break-through' in the treatment of mental illness is only a matter of time, involving as it often does further assumptions concerning the basically mechanical nature of its aetiology, may well prove extremely wasteful if other possibilities are not also borne in mind.

The results of such research, together with a consideration of the kind of evidence put forward in this book, could conceivably lead to the questioning of a number of basic assumptions which are now found in such areas as, for example, the training of psychiatrists and psychiatric nurses. At present training in these fields relies largely on the transmission of attitudes which have more to do with the basic 'medical assumption' concerning the nature of mental illness than on any firmly established and scientifically validated body of knowledge about it. The medical profession, having evolved over centuries an ethical code suitable to the performance of the grave responsibilities expected of it by society, is probably the best suited to caring for the mentally ill. This does not mean, however, that traditional ideologies and approaches are *ideally* suited, nor that other disciplines have nothing to contribute, particularly to psychotherapy. On the contrary, we have argued that serious thought should be given to possible modifications in our conception of what the most reasonable scientific approach to mental illness should be.

But beyond this, the future of our understanding and treatment of mental illness is not in the hands of science alone. It depends ultimately on the valuation we place on human existence and human experience. We may choose to regard the manifestation of psychological suffering as the symptoms of illness, and we may treat these accordingly, perhaps by the indefinite, or even lifelong, administration of drugs. On the other hand, we may see such suffering in terms of the individual's intra- or inter-personal psychological experience, and we may choose to tackle the problem at this level, with such psychological techniques as psychotherapy. Whatever course we adopt, we shall be making a number of value judgments of which we may be more or less aware, and these will include social judgments about what kinds of behaviour we are going to count as acceptable and what as pathological, judgments of what constitutes happiness and effective living, judgments concerning what aspects of behaviour we should suppress and what we should try to understand.

If we are not to become hopelessly muddled in our appreciation of, and research into, the problems of mental illness (or painful psychological experience), we must subject these judgments and assumptions to the kind of searching scrutiny that we have traditionally accepted as an essential part of 'objective' science, and we must do so in order to clarify our own subjective, moral position.

References

ANTHONY, E. J. (1953) 'Group psychotherapy.' In BURTON, J. (ed.) *Group Discussion in Educational, Social and Working Life*. London: Central Council for Health Education.

BAKAN, D. (1966) 'The test of significance in psychological research.' *Psychol. Bull.*, **66**, 423–37.

BANDURA, A. (1956) 'Psychotherapists' anxiety level, self-insight, and psychotherapeutic competence.' *J. abnorm. soc. Psychol.*, **52**, 333–7.

BANNISTER, D. (1965) 'The genesis of schizophrenic thought disorder: retest of the serial invalidation hypothesis.' *Br. J. Psychiat.*, **111**, 377–82.

BANNISTER, D. (1966) 'Psychology as an exercise in paradox.' *Bull. Br. psychol. Soc.*, **19**, 21–6.

BARTON, R. (1959) *Institutional Neurosis*. Bristol: J. Wright.

BELLAK, L. (1958) *Schizophrenia: A Review of the Syndrome*. New York: Logos Press.

BERGIN, A. E. (1966) 'Some implications of psychotherapy research for therapeutic practice.' *J. abnorm. Psychol.*, **71**, 235–46.

BERGIN, A. E. and SOLOMON, S. (1963) 'Personality and performance correlates of empathic understanding in psychotherapy.' Paper read at American Psychological Association, Philadelphia, September.

BETTELHEIM, B. and SYLVESTER, E. (1948) 'A therapeutic milieu.' *Am. J. Orthopsychiat.*, **18**, 191–206.

BINSWANGER, L. (1958) 'The case of Ellen West.' In MAY, R., ANGEL, E. and ELLENBERGER, F. (eds) *Existence*. New York: Basic Books.

CAINE, T. M. (1963) 'Response suppression in normal and psychotic groups.' *Psychol. Rep.*, **12**, 942.

CAINE, T. M. (1964) 'Personality tests for nurses.' *Nursing Times*, 24 July, 973–4.

CAINE, T. M. (1965) 'Changes in symptom, attitude and trait measures among chronic neurotics in a therapeutic community.' In FOULDS, G. A. *Personality and Personal Illness*. London: Tavistock.

CAINE, T. M. (1966) 'Perceptual sensitization, response suppression and psychopathology.' *Br. J. Psychol.*, **57**, 301–6.

CAINE, T. M. (in press) 'Personality and illness.' In MITTLER, P. (ed.) *Psychological Assessments*. London: Methuen.

CAINE, T. M. and HOPE, K. (1967) *Manual of the Hysteroid-Obsessoid Questionnaire (HOQ)*. London: University of London Press Ltd.

CAINE, T. M. and SMAIL, D. J. (1966) 'Attitudes to treatment of medical staff in therapeutic communities.' *Br. J. med. Psychol.*, **39**, 329–34.

CAINE, T. M. and SMAIL, D. J. (1967*a*) 'Attitudes of psychiatrists to staff roles and treatment methods.' *Br. J. med. Psychol.*, **40**, 179–82.

CAINE, T. M. and SMAIL, D. J. (1967*b*) 'Personal relevance and the choice of constructs for the repertory grid technique.' *Br. J. Psychiat.*, **113**, 517–20.

CAINE, T. M. and SMAIL, D. J. (1968*a*) 'Attitudes of psychiatric nurses to their role in treatment.' *Br. J. med. Psychol.*, **41**, 193–7.

CAINE, T. M. and SMAIL, D. J. (1968*b*) 'Attitudes of psychiatric patients to staff roles and treatment methods in mental hospitals.' *Br. J. med. Psychol.*, **41**, 291–4.

CAINE, T. M., CHICK, J. R. and SMAIL, D. J. (1967) 'Personality attributes of occupational therapists.' *Occup. Therapy*, **30**, 25–7.

CAINE, T. M., FOULDS, G. A. and HOPE, K. (1967) *Manual of the Hostility and Direction of Hostility Questionnaire (HDHQ)*. London: University of London Press Ltd.

CAMPBELL, D. (1960) 'The psychological effects of cerebral electroshock.' In EYSENCK, H. J. (ed.) *Handbook of Abnormal Psychology*. London: Methuen.

CANTRIL, H., AMES, A., HASTORF, A. H. and ITTLESON, W. H. (1949) 'Psychology and scientific research. I. The nature of scientific inquiry.' *Science*, **110**.

CARTWRIGHT, R. D. and LERNER, B. (1963) 'Empathy, need to change, and improvement with psychotherapy.' *J. consult. Psychol.*, **27**, 138–44.

CATTELL, R. B. and EBER, H. W. (1957) *Handbook of the Sixteen Personality Factor Questionnaire.* Champaign, Illinois: Institute for Personality and Ability Testing.

CHERTOK, L. (1966) 'An introduction to the study of tensions among psychotherapists.' *Br. J. med. Psychol.*, **39**, 237–43.

COHEN, J. and STRUENING, E. L. (1962) 'Opinions about mental illness in the personnel of two large mental hospitals.' *J. abnorm. soc. Psychol.*, **64**, 349–60.

COHEN, J. and STRUENING, E. L. (1963) 'Opinions about mental illness: mental hospital occupational profiles and profile clusters.' *Psychol. Rep.*, **12**, 111–24.

COHEN, J. and STRUENING, E. L. (1964) 'Opinions about mental illness: hospital social atmosphere and patient time in the hospital.' *J. consult. Psychol.*, **28**, 291–8.

CROCKET, R. W. (1961) 'Treatment and its results at the Ingrebourne Centre, St George's Hospital, Essex. 1 April 1957 to 31 March 1959.' Unpublished study.

CURLE, A. (1947) 'Transitional communities and social reconnection, pt 1.' *Hum. Relat.*, **1**, 42–68.

CURRAN, D. and GUTTMAN, E. (1949) *Psychological Medicine.* Edinburgh: Livingstone.

CURRAN, D. and PARTRIDGE, M. (1961) 'Psychological medicine.' In CONYBEAR, J. and MANN, W. N. (eds) *Textbook of Medicine.* Edinburgh and London: Livingstone.

DAHLSTROM, W. G. (1962) 'Commentary: the roles of social desirability and acquiescence in response to the MMPI.' In MESSICK, S. and ROSS, J. (eds) *Measurement in Personality and Cognition.* New York and London: Wiley.

DITTMAN, A. T. (1952) 'The interpersonal process in psychotherapy: development of a research method.' *J. abnorm. soc. Psychol.*, **47**, 236–44.

DOLLARD, J. and MILLER, N. E. (1950) *Personality and Psychotherapy.* New York: McGraw-Hill.

DREIKURS, R. (1955) 'Group psychotherapy and the third revolution in psychiatry.' *Int. J. soc. Psychiat.*, **1**, 23.

DUVERGER, N. (1961) *Méthode des Sciences Sociales.* Paris: Presses Universitaires de France.

EDWARDS, A. L. (1959) *Edwards Personal Preference Schedule.* New York: Psychological Corporation.

ELLSWORTH, R. B. (1965) 'A behavioral study of staff attitudes toward mental illness.' *J. abnorm. soc. Psychol.*, **70**, 194–200.

EYSENCK, H. J. (1952) 'The effects of psychotherapy: an evaluation.' *J. consult. Psychol.*, **16**, 319–24.

EYSENCK, H. J. (1959) *Behaviour Therapy and the Neuroses*. London: Pegramon.

EYSENCK, H. J. (1960) *Handbook of Abnormal Psychology*. London: Pitman.

EYSENCK, H. J. (1967) 'Intelligence assessment: a theoretical and experimental approach.' *Br. J. educ. Psychol.*, **37**, 81–98.

FIEDLER, F. E. (1950*a*) 'The concept of an ideal therapeutic relationship.' *J. consult. Psychol.*, **14**, 239–45.

FIEDLER, F. E. (1950*b*) 'A comparison of therapeutic relationships in psychoanalytic, non-directive and Adlerian therapy.' *J. consult. Psychol.*, **14**, 436–45.

FIEDLER, F. E. (1951) 'Factor analyses of psychoanalytic, non-directive and Adlerian therapeutic relationships.' *J. consult. Psychol.*, **15**, 32–8.

FISH, F. (1966) 'A concept of schizophrenia.' *Br. J. med. Psychol.*, **39**, 269–73.

FOULDS, G. A. (1959) 'The relative stability of personality measures compared with diagnostic measures.' *J. ment. Sci.*, **105**, 783–7.

FOULDS, G. A. (1965) *Personality and Personal Illness*. London: Tavistock.

FOULDS, G. A. and CAINE, T. M. (1958*a*) 'Psychoneurotic symptom clusters, trait clusters and psychological tests.' *J. ment. Sci.*, **104**, 722.

FOULDS, G. A. and CAINE, T. M. (1958*b*) 'Personality factors and performance on timed tests of ability.' *Occup. Psychol.*, **32**, 102–5.

FOULDS, G. A. and CAINE, T. M. (1959) 'Symptom clusters and personality types among psychoneurotic men compared with women.' *J. ment. Sci.*, **105**, 469.

FOULDS, G. A. and HOPE, K. (1968) *Manual of the Symptom-Sign Inventory (SSI)*. London: University of London Press Ltd.

FOULKES, S. H. and ANTHONY, E. J. (1957) *Group Psychotherapy*. Harmondsworth: Penguin Books.

FRANK, J. D., GLIEDMAN, L. H., IMBER, S. D., NASH, E. H., jr. and STONE, A. R. (1957) 'Why patients leave psychotherapy', *Archs Neurol. Psychiat.*, **77**, 283–99.

FRANK, L. K. (1948) *Society as the Patient*. New Brunswick.

FRANKEL, C. (1960) 'Philosophy and the social sciences.' In BOEWE, C. E. and NICHOLS, R. F. (eds) *Both Human and Humane*. London: Oxford University Press.

FREUD, S. (1928) *The Future of an Illusion*. London: Hogarth Press.

FREUD, S. (1949) *New Introductory Lectures on Psychoanalysis*. London: Hogarth Press.

FROMM, E. (1943) *The Fear of Freedom*. London: Allen & Unwin.

FROMM, E. (1955) *The Sane Society*. New York: Rinehart.

GERSHOY, L. (1960) 'Heritage and horizons in modern history.' In BOEWE, C. E. and NICHOLS, R. F. (eds) *Both Human and Humane*. London: Oxford University Press.

GILBERT, W. (1952) 'Counseling: therapy and diagnosis.' *Ann. Rev. Psychol.*, **3**, 351–80.

GOFFMAN, E. (1958) 'The characteristics of total institutions.' In *Symposium on Preventive and Social Psychiatry*. Washington: Walter Reid Army Institute of Research.

GROSSMAN, D. (1952) 'An experimental investigation of a psychotherapeutic technique.' *J. consult. Psychol.*, **16**, 325–31.

HALMOS, P. (1965) *The Faith of the Counsellors*. London: Constable.

HOLT, R. R. and LUBORSKY, L. (1958) *Personality Patterns of Psychiatrists*, vol. 1. London: Imago Publishing Co.

HOPE, K. (1963) 'The structure of hostility among normal and neurotic persons.' Unpublished Ph.D. thesis, University of London.

HORNEY, K. (1951) *Neurosis and Human Growth*. London: Routledge & Kegan Paul.

HUGHES, C. E. (1946) 'Institutions.' In LEE, A. M. (ed.) *New Outline of the Principles of Sociology*. New York: Barnes & Noble.

IMBER, S. D., FRANK, J., GLIEDMAN, L., NASH, E. and STONE, A. (1956) 'Suggestibility, social class, and acceptance of psychotherapy.' *J. clin. Psychol.*, **12**, 341–4.

JACKSON, D. D. (1960) *The Etiology of Schizophrenia*. New York: Basic Books.

JAQUES, E. (1951) *The Changing Culture of a Factory*. London: Tavistock.

JOHNSON, M. L. (1953) 'The ABC of group discussion: theory.' In BURTON, J. (ed.) *Group Discussion in Educational, Social and Working Life*. London: Central Council for Health Education.

JONES, M. (1952) *Social Psychiatry*. London: Tavistock.

JOURARD, S. M. (1964) *The Transparent Self*. Princeton: Van Nostrand.

JUNG, C. G. (1954) *The Practice of Psychotherapy*. Collected works, vol. 16. London: Routledge & Kegan Paul.

JUNG, C. G. (1963) *Memories, Dreams and Reflections*. London: Collins and Routledge & Kegan Paul.

KELLY, E. L. and FISKE, D. W. (1951) *The Prediction of Performance in Clinical Psychology*. Ann Arbor: University of Michigan Press.

KELLY, G. A. (1955) *The Psychology of Personal Constructs*, vols 1 and 2. New York: W. W. Norton.

KIERKEGAARD, S. (1955) *Fear and Trembling and the Sickness unto Death*. New York: Doubleday.

KIESLER, D. J. (1966) 'Some myths of psychotherapy research and the search for a paradigm.' *Psychol. Bull.*, **65**, 110–36.

KIND, H. (1966) 'The psychogenesis of schizophrenia.' *Br. J. Psychiat.*, **112**, 333–49.

KLEIN, G. S. (1958) 'Cognitive control and motivation.' In LINDZEY, G. (ed.) *Assessment of Human Motives*. New York: Rinehart.

KLINE, P. (1967) 'Obsessional traits and emotional instability.' *Br. J. med. Psychol.*, **40**, 153–7.

KOCH, S. (1964) 'Psychology and emerging conceptions of knowledge as unitary.' In WANN, T. W. (ed.) *Behaviorism and Phenomenology*. Chicago: University of Chicago Press.

KREITMAN, N. (1962) 'Psychiatric orientation: a study of attitudes among psychiatrists.' *J. ment. Sci.*, **108**, 317–28.

KUDER, G. F. (1948) *The Kuder Preference Record (Personal Form AH)*. Chicago: Science Research Associates.

LAING, R. D. (1960) *The Divided Self*. London: Tavistock.

LAING, R. D. (1967) *The Politics of Experience and the Bird of Paradise*. Harmondsworth: Penguin Books.

LAING, R. D., PHILLIPSON, H. and LEE, A. R. (1966) *Interpersonal Perception*. London: Tavistock.

LEVY, L. H. and ORR, T. B. (1959) 'The social psychology of Rorschach validity research.' *J. abnorm. soc. Psychol.*, **58**, 79–83.

LEWIS, A. J. and MAPOTHER, E. (1941) In *Price's Textbook of the Practice of Medicine*. London: Oxford University Press.

LORR, M., KATZ, M. N. and RUBINSTEIN, E. A. (1958) 'The prediction of length of stay in psychotherapy.' *J. consult. Psychol.*, **22**, 321–7.

MACALPINE, I. (1950) 'The development of the transference.' *Psychoanal. Q.*, **19**, 501–39.

MCKENZIE, J. G. (1962) *Guilt, its Meaning and Significance.* London: Allen & Unwin.

MACKINNON, D. W. (1944) 'The structure of personality.' In HUNT, J. MCV. (ed.) *Personality and the Behaviour Disorders*, vol. 1. New York: Ronald.

MARKS, I. M. and GELDER, M. G. (1966) 'Common ground between behaviour therapy and psychodynamic methods.' *Br. J. med. Psychol.*, **39**, 11–23.

MARTIN, D. V. (1955) 'Institutionalization.' *Lancet*, 1188.

MARTIN, D. V. (1962) *Adventure in Psychiatry.* Oxford: Cassirer.

MARTIN, D. V. and CAINE, T. M. (1963) 'Personality change in chronic neurotics in a therapeutic community.' *Br. J. Psychiat.*, **109**, 267.

MASLOW, A. H. (1962) *Toward a Psychology of Being.* Princeton, N.J.: Van Nostrand.

MAY, R. (1958) 'The origins and significance of the existential movement in psychology.' In MAY, R., ANGEL, E. and ELLENBERGER, F. *Existence.* New York: Basic Books.

MAY, R., ANGEL, E. and ELLENBERGER, F. (1958) *Existence.* New York: Basic Books.

MEEHL, P. E. (1954) *Clinical versus Statistical Prediction.* Minneapolis: University of Minnesota Press.

MORENO, J. L. (1952) Presidential address to the American Society of Group Psychotherapy and Psychodrama. New York.

MORRIS, C. (1956) *Variations of Human Values.* Chicago: University of Chicago Press.

MORRIS, C., EIDUSON, B. and O'DONOVAN, D. (1960) 'Values of psychiatric patients.' *Behavl Sci.*, **5**, 297–312.

MOWBRAY, R. M. and RODGER, T. F. (1963) *Psychology in relation to Medicine.* Edinburgh and London: Livingstone.

MOWRER, O. H. (1961) *The Crisis in Psychiatry and Religion.* Princeton, N.J.: Van Nostrand.

MYERS, I. B. (1962) *Manual of the Myers–Briggs Type Indicator.* Princeton, N.J.: Educational Testing Service.

MYRDAL, G. (1958) *Value in Social Theory.* London: Routledge & Kegan Paul.

PIPPARD, J. (1966) 'Therapeutic community—why bother?' Paper read at Purdysburn Hospital, Belfast, 6 December.

POLANYI, M. (1958) *Personal Knowledge*. London: Routledge & Kegan Paul.

RAPOPORT, R. N. (1960) *Community as Doctor*. London: Tavistock.

REVANS, R. W. (1964) *Standards for Morale. Cause and Effect in Hospitals*. Published for the Nuffield Provincial Hospitals Trust. London: Oxford University Press.

ROGERS, C. R. (1957) 'The necessary and sufficient conditions of therapeutic personality change.' *J. consult. Psychol.*, **21**, 95–103.

ROGERS, C. R. (1961) *On Becoming a Person*. London: Constable.

ROSENBERG, C. M. (1967) 'Personality and obsessional neurosis.' *Br. J. Psychiat.*, **113**, 471–7.

ROSENTHAL, D. (1955) 'Changes in some moral values following psychotherapy.' *J. consult. Psychol.*, **19**, 431–6.

ROSENZWEIG, S. (1954) 'A transvaluation of psychotherapy: a reply to Hans Eysenck.' *J. abnorm. soc. Psychol.*, **49**, 298–304.

RUBINSTEIN, E. A. and LORR, M. (1956) 'A comparison of terminators and remainers in outpatient psychotherapy.' *J. clin. Psychol.*, **12**, 345–9.

RUBINSTEIN, E. A. and PARLOFF, M. B. (1959) *Research in Psychotherapy*, vol. 1. Washington: American Psychological Association.

SALZMAN, L. (1966) 'Memory and psychoanalysis.' *Br. J. med. Psychol.*, **39**, 197–206.

SAWYER, J. (1966) 'Measurement and prediction, clinical and statistical.' *Psychol. Bull.*, **66**, 178–200.

SCOTT, R. D. and ASHWORTH, P. L. (1965) 'The "axis value" and the transfer of psychosis. A scored analysis of the interaction in the families of schizophrenic patients.' *Br. J. med. Psychol.*, **38**, 97–116.

SCRIVEN, M. (1964) 'Views of human nature.' In WANN, T. W. (ed.) *Behaviorism and Phenomenology*. Chicago: University of Chicago Press.

SEARLES, H. F. (1965) *Collected Papers on Schizophrenia and Related Subjects*. London: Hogarth Press.

SHAPIRO, M. B. (1951) 'An experimental approach to diagnostic psychological testing.' *J. ment. Sci.*, **97**, 748–64.

SHOENBERG, E. (ed.) (in press) *A Hospital Looks at Itself. Claybury Patients and Staff and the Making of a Therapeutic Community*. Oxford: Cassirer.

SLATER, E. (1950) 'The genetical aspects of personality and neurosis.' *Congrès Internationale de Psychiatrie, Paris. VI, Psychiatrie Sociale, Génétique et Eugénique.*

SLATER, E. and P. (1944) 'A heuristic theory of neurosis.' *J. neurol. Psychiat.*, **7**, 49.

SMAIL, D. J. (1966) 'A multiple-choice version of the TAT as a measure of aggression in psychiatric patients.' *Br. J. med. Psychol.*, **39**, 163–9.

SMAIL, D. J. (1968) 'The place of conscious experience in clinical and medical psychology.' *Br. J. med. Psychol.*, **41**, 169–76.

SNYGG, D. and COMBS, A. W. (1949) *Individual Behavior: A New Frame of Reference for Psychology.* New York: Harper Bros.

SOROKIN, P. A. (1956) *Fads and Foibles in Modern Sociology and Related Sciences.* Chicago: Henry Regnery.

STRUPP, H. H. (1958*a*) 'The performance of psychoanalytic and client-centred therapists in an initial interview.' *J. consult. Psychol.*, **22**, 265–74.

STRUPP, H. H. (1958*b*) 'The performance of psychiatrists and psychologists in a therapeutic interview.' *J. clin. Psychol.*, **14**, 219–26.

STRUPP, H. H. (1960) 'The nature of the therapist's contribution to treatment process.' *Archs gen. Psychiat.*, **3**, 219–31.

STRUPP, H. H. (1962) 'Patient–doctor relationships: the psychotherapist in the therapeutic process.' In BACHRACH, A. J. (ed.) *Experimental Foundations of Clinical Psychology.* New York: Basic Books.

STRUPP, H. H., WALLACH, M. S. and WOGAN, M. (1964) 'Psychotherapy experience in retrospect: questionnaire survey of former patients and their therapists.' *Psychol. Monogr.*, **78**, no. 11, whole no. 588.

SULLIVAN, H. S. (1953) *The Interpersonal Theory of Psychiatry.* New York: Norton; London: Tavistock.

SULLIVAN, P. L., MILLER, C. and SMELSER, W. (1958) 'Factors in length of stay and progress in psychotherapy.' *J. consult. Psychol.*, **22**, 1–9.

SUNDBERG, N. D. and TYLER, L. E. (1963) *Clinical Psychology.* London: Methuen.

TIENARI, P. (1963) *Psychiatric Illness in Identical Twins.* Copenhagen: Munksgaard.

TRUAX, C. B. (1961) 'A scale for the measurement of accurate empathy.' *Psychiat. Inst. Bull.* Wisconsin Psychiatric Institute, University of Wisconsin, Madison, Wis., **12**, 1.

TRUAX, C. B. (1962*a*) 'A tentative scale for the measurement of therapist genuineness or self-congruence.' *Discussion Papers,* Wisconsin Psychiatric Institute, University of Wisconsin, Madison, Wis., **35**.

TRUAX, C. B. (1962*b*) 'A tentative scale for the measurement of unconditional positive regard.' *Psychiat. Inst. Bull.* Wisconsin Psychiatric Institute, University of Wisconsin, Madison, Wis., **1**, 2.

TRUAX, C. B. (1963) Effective ingredients in psychotherapy: an approach to unravelling the patient–therapist interaction. *J. counsel. Psychol.*, **3**, 256.

TRUAX, C. B. and WARGO, D. G. (1966) 'Psychotherapeutic encounters that change behaviour: for better or for worse.' *Am. J. Psychother.*, **20**, 499–520.

TRUAX, C. B. *et al.* (1966*a*) 'Therapist empathy, genuineness, and warmth and patient therapeutic outcome.' *J. consult. Psychol.*, **30**, 395–401.

TRUAX, C. B., WARGO, D. G. and SILBER, L. D. (1966*b*) 'Effects of group psychotherapy with high accurate empathy and non-possessive warmth upon female institutionalized delinquents.' *J. abnorm. Psychol.*, **4**, 267–74.

WALTON, H. J. (1966) 'Differences between physically-minded and psychologically-minded medical practitioners.' *Br. J. Psychiat.*, **112**, 1097–102.

WALTON, H. J. and HOPE, K. (1967) 'The effect of age and personality on doctors' clinical preferences.' *Br. J. soc. clin. Psychol.*, **6**, 43–51.

WELKOWITZ, J., COHEN, J. and ORTMEYER, D. (1967) 'Value system similarity: investigation of patient–therapist dyads.' *J. consult. Psychol.*, **31**, 48–55.

WHITE, V. (1952) *God and the Unconscious.* London: Harvill Press.

WHITE, V. (1960) *Soul and Psyche.* London: Collins and Harvill Press.

WHITEHORN, J. C. and BETZ, B. J. (1954) 'A study of the psychotherapeutic relationships between physicians and schizophrenic patients.' *Am. J. Psychiat.*, **111**, 321–31.

WING, J. K. (1962) 'Institutionalization in mental hospitals.' *Br. J. soc. clin. Psychol.*, **1**, 38–51.

WOLF, E. (1966) 'Learning theory and psychoanalysis.' *Br. J. med. Psychol.*, **39**, 1–10.

WOLPE, J. (1962) 'The experimental foundations of some new psychotherapeutic methods.' In BACHRACH, A. J. (ed.) *Experimental Foundations of Clinical Psychology.* New York: Basic Books.

WOLPE, J., SALTER, S. and REYNA, L. (1964) *The Conditioning Therapies.* New York: Holt, Rinehart & Winston.

WOOTTON, B. (1960) *Social Science and Social Pathology.* London: Allen & Unwin.

World Health Organisation Expert Committee on Mental Health (1953) Quoted in CLARK, D. (1964) *Administrative Therapy.* London: Tavistock.

ZILBOORG, G. and HENRY, G. A. (1941) *A History of Medical Psychology.* New York: Norton.

Index

acceptance, 54, 148
acting out hostility, 106, 108
alienation, 48
Allport–Vernon study of values, 144
anality, 43
analytical psychology, 37
Anthony, E. J., 46, 47
anxiety, 147, 151
  state, 104, 106
assumptions
  in organic psychiatry, 30
  in psychoanalysis, 33
  in science, 23
  in treatment philosophies, 28, 34, 84, 166
  medical, 30, 32, 173
atmosphere
  in hospitals, 84, 85, 168
  therapeutic, 84, 102
attitudes, 102
attitudes to treatment, 59, 87, 168
  of nurses, 71, 76, 85
  of patients, 79, 82
  of psychiatrists, 66, 84, 85, 88
authority, 74
  of doctors, 70, 72
authoritarianism, 78, 85, 96, 100, 140

Bacon, Francis, 45
Bakan, D., 155
Bandura, A., 146, 151
Bannister, D., 90, 160, 161
Barton, R., 47
behaviour therapy, 25, 26, 28, 133
behaviourism, 28, 155
Bellak, L., 30
Bergin, A. E., 59, 135, 150, 151
Bettelheim, B., 48
Betz, B. J., 146
Binswanger, L., 31, 32, 42, 43
Bruno, Giordano, 45
Buber, M., 41

Caine, T. M., 8, 47, 60, 70, 78, 91, 100, 102, 103, 104, 105, 106, 109, 114, 125, 161, 163
Campbell, D., 31
Cantril, H., 47
Cartwright, R. D., 142, 148
Cattell, R. B., 89, 90, 96, 171
Cattell 16-PF test, 89, 92, 95, 97, 99, 171
Chertok, L., 26, 70
Chick, J. R., 100
Civil Resettlement units, 49, 56
Claybury Hospital, 54, 57, 59
client-centred therapy, 147
Cohen, J., 84, 85, 145
Combs, A. W., 158
communalism, 51, 57
communication, 52, 54, 78, 80
comparative treatment, 171
  sample, 112, 118

component 1, 171
  of doctors, 66, 86, 88, 92, 97, 99, 113
  of nurses, 72, 113
  of patients, 80
component 2
  of doctors, 67
  of nurses, 72
  of patients, 80
component 3
  of doctors, 67
  of nurses, 72, 74
  of patients, 81
concern, 54, 81
confession, 41
conflict, between staff members, 168
congruence, 147, 149
conscientiousness, 96
conscious appraisal, 167
conscious experience, 158
consciousness, 54, 154
constructs, in repertory grid technique, 90
conventional treatment, 101, 121, 124
corrective emotional experience, 140, 158
crisis, emotional, 112, 162
criticism of others, 106, 108
Crocket, R. W., 55
culture
  and medicine, 14
  and neurosis, 47
  and science, 23
  in mental hospitals, 84
Curle, A., 48, 49
Curran, D., 104

Dahlstrom, W. G., 163
Daseinsanalyse, 41, 43
defence mechanisms, 33
democratic outlook, 96
democratic processes in treatment, 49, 50
democratization, 50, 57
discipline, 72, 80, 89, 140, 172
distance
  emotional, 138
  psychological, 48, 70, 73, 77, 81
Dittman, A. T., 141, 142
doctor–patient relationship, 15, 35, 52, 70, 146
  in analytical psychology, 38
  in behaviour therapy, 26
  in existential analysis, 42
  in organic psychiatry, 25
  in psychoanalysis, 26
  in therapeutic communities, 52, 112
Dollard, J., 29
Dreikurs, R., 45
drugs, 31, 58, 112, 113, 121, 124, 169
Duverger, N., 19, 22
dysthymia, 104, 106, 115

Eber, H. W., 89, 96, 171
Edwards, A. L., 150
Edwards Personal Preference Schedule, 150
effectiveness of treatments, 55, 58, 85, 137
ego strength, 125, 142
electro-convulsive therapy, 31, 117
Ellsworth, R. B., 86
emotional stability, 96
empathy, 20, 99, 139, 140, 147, 148, 149, 157, 170
Erasmus, 45
evaluation of treatment, 102
evidence, in psychology, 157
evil, problem of, 40
existential analysis, 41, 150
existentialism, 41, 165
  and psychoanalysis, 43
extraversion–introversion, 97
Eysenck, H. J., 28, 31, 58, 59, 134, 135, 163

failures, in treatment, 116, 125
faith, 19, 169
  healing, 14

fashion, in treatment, 31
feeling, expression of, 54, 111
Fiedler, F. E., 138
Fish, F., 30
Fiske, D. W., 164
follow-up
  one year, 114
  five years, 117
Foulds, G. A., 20, 103, 104, 106, 109, 163
Foulkes, S. H., 46, 47
Frank, J. D., 142
Frank, L. K., 46
Frankel, C., 20, 21, 22, 23
Freud, S., 33, 34, 36, 38, 39, 43, 45, 46, 139, 159
Fromm, E., 46, 47

Gelder, M. G., 29
genuineness, 99, 147, 149, 157, 171
Gershoy, L., 22
Gilbert, W., 136
Goffman, E., 47, 48
Grossman, D., 141
Guildford–Martin Personality Inventory, 97, 98, 171
guilt, 18, 40, 106, 108, 122
Guttman, E., 104

Halmos, P., 16, 18, 26, 35, 46, 198
Heidegger, M., 41
Henderson Hospital, 56
Henry, G. A., 14, 15, 45
Holt, R. R., 99, 147, 164
Hope, K., 9, 100, 106, 163
Horney, K., 47
hostility, 106, 122
  amount of, 106
  direction of, 106
Hostility and Direction of Hostility Questionnaire (HDHQ), 108, 116
Hughes, C. E., 12
Hume, D., 44
hysteria, 103, 107, 115
hysterical personality, 104
hysterical symptoms, 104
hysteroid component of personality, 104, 107, 115
Hysteroid-Obsessoid Questionnaire (HOQ), 107, 115, 122

Imber, S. D., 142
Ingrebourne Centre, 55
insight, 96, 98, 100, 141, 147, 170
institutionalization, 48, 52
interests, of nurses, 78
interpretations, 111, 123, 140, 141
involvement, 77, 110, 158
Ittré, Emile, 14

Jackson, D. D., 30, 31
James, W., 24
Janet, P., 103, 104
Jaques, E., 47, 171
Johnson, M. L., 47
Jones, M., 50
Jourard, S. M., 27, 70, 150, 171
Jung, C. G., 18, 37, 38, 39, 40, 41, 97, 150

Katz, M. N., 142
Kelly, E. L., 164
Kelly, G. A., 90, 142, 158, 164
Kierkegaard, S., 41, 43
Kiesler, D. J., 58, 134, 164
Kind, H., 32, 33
King Edward's Hospital Fund, 172
Kirkwood, R., 9
Klein, G. S., 162
Kline, P., 104
Koch, S., 28, 44
Kraepelin, E., 33
Kreitman, N., 88, 97, 98, 99, 171
Kuder, G. F., 171
Kuder Preference Record, 78, 100, 171

Laing, R. D., 31, 42, 165
learning theory, 28
Lerner, B., 142, 148
leucotomy, 31, 58
Levy, L. H., 8
Lewis, A. J., 104
Locke, J., 44
Lorr, M., 142
love, 18, 20, 26
Luborsky, L., 99, 147, 164

Macalpine, I., 139
McKenzie, J. G., 18
Mackinnon, D. W., 103
magic
  and medicine, 14
  and science, 85
Mapother, E., 104
Marks, I. M., 29
Martin, D. V., 47, 53, 54, 56, 59, 78, 109
Maslow, A. H., 36
materialism, medical, 24, 39
Maudsley Hospital, 98
May, R., 23, 42
meaning, 167
mechanism, 42, 134, 159, 167
  in mental illness, 25
  in psychoanalysis, 34, 43
  in science, 24
medicine
  and moral problems, 40
  and science, 15
  history of, 14
  physical, 171
Meehl, P. E., 164
mental health
  and politics, 46
  and value judgments, 16, 17
  definitions of, 16
mental illness
  aetiology of, 12, 24, 30, 172
  and criminality, 16
  and physical illness, 11, 12, 16, 162
  and religion, 38
  meaning of, 41
  opinions about, 85
Mill Hill Vocabulary Scale, 114
Miller, C., 143
Miller, N. E., 29
Minnesota Multiphasic Personality Inventory (MMPI), 97, 115, 118, 150
Mooney Problem Check List, 115, 116
More, Thomas, 45
Moreno, J. L., 45
Morris, C., 144
Mowbray, R. M., 12, 26
Mowrer, O. H., 40, 41
Myers, I. B., 171
Myers–Briggs Type Indicator, 171
Myrdal, G., 20
mysticism, 36, 37
myths in psychotherapy, 134, 164

natural science, 21, 32, 33, 88, 154, 166
need to change, 142
neurotic depression, 104, 107
neuroticism, 96, 99, 100, 169
neutrality, 26, 136, 153, 158
Northfield Army Neurosis Centre, 47
nurse–patient relationship, 73, 85

objectivism, 16, 17, 22, 42, 166, 172
obsessive-compulsive states, 104, 107
obsessoid component of personality, 104, 107, 115
occupational therapists, 100, 110, 111, 168
orality, 43
Orr, T. B., 8
Ortmeyer, D., 145
outcome of treatment, 133, 136, 146, 153

Parloff, M. B., 137
participation, 50, 112, 141

paternalism, 85
permissiveness, 51, 53, 54, 57
Personal Disturbance Scale, 115, 118
personality
change, conditions of, 147
disorder, 116, 122
inadequate, 116
measures, 115, 121
of doctors, 56, 71, 87, 99, 111, 168
of nurses, 78, 111, 168
of therapists, 137, 157
schizoid, 116
trait constellations, 105
traits, 103, 109
type, 106, 125
phenomenology, 31, 43, 165
Pippard, J., 54
Polanyi, M., 36
positivism, 44, 155
Price, E. J. J., 9
process in psychotherapy, 136, 138
projected hostility, 106, 108
psychasthenia, 104
psychiatric social workers, 110
psychiatry, 88
and social science, 20
as a profession, 12
diagnosis in, 31, 106
eclectic, 25
organic, 25, 30, 31
revolutions in, 45
values in, 54
psychoanalysis, 26, 29, 33, 41, 43, 99, 139, 158
psychological tests
and prediction, 164
as objective measuring instruments, 161
personal relevance of, 163
psychologists
and psychiatrists, 140
industrial, 171
psychology
experimental, 160
methodology in, 155, 165
psychopathology, 24, 32, 37, 40, 167
psychotherapy, 25, 58, 101, 102, 111, 113, 121, 125, 134, 135
effectiveness of, 58
group, 47, 68
individual, 47, 68
psychotic depressives, 117
psychotics, 122

questionnaire of attitudes to treatment, 59, 87, 171
construction of, 59
items of, 61
principal components of, 65
validation of principal components of, 68

Rapoport, R. N., 45, 50, 51, 54, 145
reality confrontation, 50, 51, 57
reductionism, 19, 32, 41, 42, 159
reflection of feeling, 140, 142, 151
regard, positive, 147, 149
rehabilitation, 50, 52, 55
relationships (*see also* doctor–patient *and* nurse–patient relationship)
family, 110
in hospital, 124
in therapeutic communities, 51, 110
psychotherapeutic, 18, 26, 53, 77, 136, 138, 150, 157, 166, 170
staff, 53, 55, 70, 167
staff–patient, 53, 73, 80, 113, 167
religion, 18, 33, 37, 39, 54
repertory grid technique, 90, 93, 95, 142, 148, 164
research
in psychiatry, 31, 58, 170, 172
in psychotherapy, 58, 102
in therapeutic communities, 59

responsibility, 54, 112
Revans, R. W., 47, 78, 85, 171
Reyna, L., 133
Rodger, T. F., 12, 26
Rogers, C. R., 20, 42, 147, 148, 150
roles, staff, 54, 81, 82, 89, 112, 148
Rosenberg, C. M., 104
Rosenthal, D., 144, 145
Rosenzweig, S., 135
Rubinstein, E. A., 137, 142

Salter, S., 133
Salzman, L., 159, 160
sampling techniques, 156
Sartre, J.-P., 41
Sawyer, J., 164
schizophrenia, 13, 30, 42
  genetic basis of, 30
  psychological factors in, 32
schools of psychotherapy
  Adlerian, 138
  Rogerian, 138, 139
  psychoanalytic, 138, 139
science
  and determinism, 20
  and mechanism, 24
  applied, 35
  in existentialism, 42
  in psychiatric treatment, 34, 77
  in psychoanalysis, 33
  truth in, 20
Scott, R. D., 165
Scriven, M., 154
Searles, H. F., 143
selection
  of patients, 113
  of staff, 56, 77, 78, 85
self-criticism, 106, 108
self-knowledge, 41
sensitivity, 96, 100, 170
Shapiro, M. B., 164
Shoenberg, E., 54
sin, 41
sincerity, 49, 53
Slater, E., 104
Slater, P., 104
Smail, D. J., 8, 60, 70, 91, 100, 158, 162, 163
Smelser, W., 143
Snygg, D., 158
social ambition, and the repertory grid, 95
Social Rehabilitation Unit, 50, 51, 145
social science, 19, 20, 154, 166
  and natural science, 21
  applied, 35
Solomon, S., 150, 151
Sorokin, P. A., 22
Spearman, C., 91
spontaneous remission, 135
statistics
  and behaviour therapy, 29
  and psychology, 155
Strong Vocational Interest Blank, 145
Struening, E. L., 84, 85
Strupp, H., 137, 139, 140, 141, 142, 143, 151, 152
subjectivity, 159
successes, in treatment, 116, 170
Sullivan, H. S., 47
Sullivan, P. L., 143
Sundberg, N. D., 7, 137
superego, 41
Sylvester, E., 48
symptom
  complexes, 104
  measures, 115, 121
Symptom-Sign Inventory (SSI), 106, 115, 163
symptoms, 103, 109

taboo against tenderness, 172
technique, in psychotherapy, 27, 42, 137, 138, 139, 140, 141, 148, 151, 153, 157
technology, 35
tender-mindedness, 19, 100, 156, 170
Thematic Apperception Test (TAT), 162

therapeutic community, 45, 59, 68, 109
as transitional communities, 47
beliefs concerning, 51
effectiveness of, 55
principles of, 49, 50
treatment of neurosis, 47
thinking introversion, 98, 100, 170
Tienari, P., 31
Tillich, P., 41
total institutions, 47, 48
tough-mindedness, 19, 96, 156, 170
traditional
doctors, 56, 81
hospitals, 169
mental hospitals, 56
nurses, 56, 72, 81, 169
training
and personality, 97
of doctors, 71, 87, 168, 173
of nurses, 77, 168, 173
of therapists, 148
transference, 26, 46, 54, 110, 139, 151
traumata, psychic, 32
treatment
as a mechanical process, 71
psychological, 50
treatment orientations, 24
and personality, 97
eclectic, 68
group psychotherapy, 68
individual psychotherapy, 68
philosophic/religious, 37
physical treatments, 68, 80, 88, 96
scientific, 25
theories of, 35
therapeutic community, 68, 83, 88, 96
Truax, C. B., 149, 150, 152, 171
Tyler, L. E., 7, 137

unconscious, the, 158

value judgments
and mental health, 16, 17, 25
and psychotherapy, 36, 99, 101, 133, 166
and science, 36, 166
and social science, 20
values, moral, 144
Vives, Juan, 45

Wallach, M. S., 151, 152
Walton, H. J., 100
Wargo, D. G., 149, 150
warmth, 54, 139, 140, 149, 157, 171
Ways to Live scale, 145
Welkowitz, J., 145
White, Ann, 9
White, V., 37, 40
Whitehorn, J. C., 154
Wing, J. K., 48
Wogan, M., 151, 152
Wolf, E., 158
Wolpe, J., 29, 133
Wootton, B., 16, 17
word association, 37
World Health Organisation, 54

Zilboorg, G., 14, 15, 45